AZTEC PRISON ART PAÑOS

Eric "Superman" Sturgess

Rose Of Sharon
PUBLISHING

ERIC "SUPERMAN" STURGESS

Printed Worldwide
First Printing 2025
First Edition 2025

10 9 8 7 6 5 4 3 2 1

Rose of Sharon Publishing books may be ordered through booksellers or by contacting:

Rose Of Sharon Publishing
roseofsharonpublishing.com
P.O. Box 186
Floresville, Texas 78114

ISBN: 978-1-970335-23-1 Paperback

Dedication

This book is a heartfelt dedication to the men in the California Department of Corrections and Rehabilitation, as well as those in prisons across America, who are striving to improve themselves and reunite with their loved ones. Within the confines of those prison walls, many men have been blessed with remarkable talents, and they take great pride in their creations and the stories they have to share. This humble book serves as a platform for their voices to be heard.

I have taken it upon myself to write numerous letters of support for resentencing and parole board hearings on behalf of my incarcerated friends in the California Department of Corrections and Rehabilitation. I am fully committed to assisting in their release, and these letters of support play a crucial role in that endeavor.

"The Lord has given them special skills as engravers, designers, embroiderers in blue, purple, and scarlet thread on fine linen cloth, and weavers. They excel as craftsmen and as designers," Exodus 35:35.

God bless you,
Eric "Superman" Sturgess
Psalm 91

Foreword

My name is Isaac Morquecho. I was born in Nezahualcóyotl, Mexico, on October 19, 1982. The book is like no other in the world. This book compiles multiple art pieces done by California prison system residents who love and honor their Mexican roots like mine.
When I was a little kid in Mexico, I fell in love with my culture. The Aztecs, Mexicas, Olmecas, Toltecas, Mayans, Chichimecas, and many other indigenous tribes lived in Mexico and continue to do so today. Learning about my roots was vital because it helped me understand my origins.

I remember, as a kid, how my parents pushed education on me and how, in the middle of their financial struggles, they always found a way to afford my school uniform, books, school materials, and even the school field trips I took to historical sites such as The Piramides de Teotihuacan, and the state of Guanajuato, Mexico, "Cuna de la Revolucion Mexicana."
The first time I visited the Pyramids of Teotihuacan in central Mexico, I was amazed by their beauty and grandeur. I could not imagine or fathom how my ancestors could have developed and built such beautiful and impressive temples in Teotihuacan and throughout my country. The advanced engineering, architecture, mathematical, and astronomical knowledge they possessed was terrific and always intrigued me. I was amazed by their myths and legends, such as those of Cuauhtémoc, Moctezuma, Huitzilopochtli, Mexicatl, Quetzalcoatl, Popocatepetl, and Iztlacihuatl. These stories portrayed a culture developed by warriors and individuals who displayed courage, honor, strength, loyalty, and discipline, as well as love and care for their Calpollis (families).

Unfortunately, our California gang culture and prison system have cast a negative and criminal stigma over our Aztec and Mexica culture, in which our ancient stories and symbolisms have been manipulated to represent criminal mindsets. Individuals have negatively portrayed our ancestors' stories, bravery, and symbols. As a native Mexican, I believe we can not continue to show our Mexican culture in that manner.

Therefore, Eric "Superman" Sturgess and I have come to present you with this book, in which residents from all over the California prison system have blasted their love for their culture on paper and cloth. We invite you to look at these pieces of art with an open mind and to look at the symbolism with love and respect for a culture that was oppressed, violated, and destroyed by the greed of the Spanish conquistadors. Our heritage continues to suffer due to the negative and criminal stigma that has been cast upon it by California's gangs and prison system.

Our Aztec roots are part of our Mexican heritage, and as a proud Mexican, I will honor them through my art and the spiritual principles they left us in their stories and legends. Courage, Loyalty, Honor, Family, Love, and Respect. Disfruta nuestra Herencia Azteca.

Paño Collection

For more than 15 years, I have been collecting paños and currently possess a collection of over 500. It is safe to say that my paño collection is the most extensive and up-to-date in the world. Through my connections with numerous inmate artists in the California Department of Corrections and Rehabilitation (CDCR), I am able to directly purchase their paños. In the past few months alone, I have generously contributed tens of thousands of dollars to both inmates in the CDCR and their family members in exchange for their artistic creations. The inmates themselves determine the method of payment they prefer, whether it be through depositing money into their trust account or transferring funds directly to their family members via Cash App, Zelle, or PayPal. Some inmates even request that I purchase quarterly or special packages for them, providing me with a list of the items they require.

While I am open to special requests for paños, I typically encourage the artists to draw what they excel at. It is important to me that I do not hinder their artistic abilities by asking them to create something outside of their comfort zone. Over time, I have developed friendships with several inmates, and we engage in daily conversations. These men take great pride in the paños they create, often carrying their finished masterpieces around the prison to showcase them to individuals they are close to. For example, before my friend Downer sent out my paño, he proudly displayed it to his teachers, group facilitators, and friends on the prison yard.

Downer expressed, "I dedicated so much time to creating this paño; it feels like letting go of my own child. I truly love this piece, and I am confident that you will appreciate it as well. I took it to my art class, and a lady from San Diego State University saw it and absolutely loved it. Even the sergeant was present and asked me numerous questions about it. He even expressed interest in displaying some of my artwork on the lockers in the dayroom."

Table of Contents

Introduction

Within the confines of incarceration, a distinct form of expression emerged, casting its shadow on the walls of jails and prisons. The tale of paños intertwines ingenuity, perseverance, and the innate human desire to communicate, surpassing the barriers of confinement. These small fabric fragments hold a profound history that unveils the intricate tapestry of life behind bars. From these seemingly unassuming beginnings, sparked by the yearning to draw and convey, a remarkable art form was born.

The term paño, meaning cloth, encompassed more than its literal definition. It became a conduit for prisoners to convey personal messages to others. A birthday paño adorned with delicate flowers, birthdates, and names became a heartfelt connection between incarcerated loved ones and their families on the outside. There is a poetic quality in inmates utilizing a paño, a mere piece of cloth, to tangibly represent their emotions and send them to their loved ones.

Beyond individual narratives, paños took on a collective identity. They symbolized affiliations, serving as a visual representation of gang allegiances. Religious iconography also found its place on these miniature canvases, capturing the spiritual yearnings of those behind bars.

As time passed, the paño evolved from its utilitarian origins into a canvas for intricate and deeply personal artistry. No longer confined to mere communication, these cloth fragments transformed into windows into the souls of their creators. These exquisite works of art reveal emotions, stories, and glimpses of a world many had never known.

Many paño artists have conveyed to me their belief that drawing serves as a meditative practice. The act of creating art allows them to find solace and alleviate stress. Whenever they experience feelings of sadness, frustration, or any other negative emotions, these artists instinctively reach for their pens and begin drawing, liberating their minds from the burdens that weigh them down.

Numerous incarcerated artists possess distinct approaches to preparing their paños in order to absorb ink from their pens. Some opt to briefly soak their paño in milk before affixing it to a wall. While the paño is attached to the wall, artists may utilize their hands or prison identification cards to eliminate any air bubbles. Subsequently, they allow the paño to remain on the wall for several hours until it becomes rigid, resembling thick construction paper. Once the paño has fully dried, they carefully peel it off the wall.

By adhering to this preparation technique, the drawing process becomes more convenient for these artists. Some argue that milk enhances the fabric's ink absorption capacity, resulting in a smoother application. Alternatively, certain incarcerated artists prepare the paño using floor wax, similar to the milk method. Ultimately, the choice between milk and floor wax depends on the artist's personal preference and the availability of these materials.

In the following pages, we embark on a journey through the artistry of paños. We delve into the stories they tell, the emotions they encapsulate, and the resilience they represent. Join us as we unravel the threads of creativity woven within the confines of captivity and discover the power of paños to transcend the limitations of their origin.

Artists' Statements

The exploration of paños would not be fully comprehensive without recognizing the invaluable contributions made by incarcerated individuals within the California Department of Corrections and Rehabilitation. These individuals have greatly enhanced my understanding of the art of drawing within the confines of prison, as well as the significance of sharing their creations with the outside world.

With a combined experience of over 60 years within the California Department of Corrections and Rehabilitation, they possess a wealth of knowledge and insight. My dedication to accuracy in the development of this book remains steadfast, and it is crucial to acknowledge that its completion would have been unattainable without the eloquent voices that have served as my inspiration.

Through the profound statements of these inmates, we are able to gain a glimpse into their artistic expression and delve into the impact that these artworks have on their lives within the prison walls. Their stories of resilience, creativity, and the transformative power of art continue to inspire me.

Inmate Artist: Downer

It is difficult to determine the exact time and place of the first paño created in a California prison. However, it is evident that this form of art has been an integral part of California Chicano prison culture for several decades, possibly even a century. The initial Chicano gangs in the United States emerged in the 1920s in the East Side of Los Angeles, and during that time, individuals would draw. Consequently, it becomes a challenge to identify the originator, date, or location of the first paño.

Nevertheless, what can be ascertained about the history of paños is that it has existed for a significant period. For generations, individuals in prison have repurposed their new sheets, pillowcases, and prison boxers by cutting them to obtain a fresh piece of white fabric for creating their paños. This process has been passed down from one generation of individuals in the California prison system to the next.

Creating a paño using state property, such as sheets, pillowcases, and boxers, is against the rules and regulations of the institution. Individuals can face disciplinary action, such as a 115 RVR, for damaging state property. The consequences for such infractions may include the loss of credits for up to 90 days, a 30-60 day loss of privileges, and in some cases, individuals may even be charged for destroying state property. Nevertheless, despite these potential repercussions, we persist in creating paños as a means of self-expression.

The roots of our paño drawings can be traced back to our indigenous heritage. Chicano prison culture was established and developed due to our pride and ongoing connection to our Mexica and Azteca roots. In the prehispanic era, the Nahuatlecos would draw and document their war stories, history, rulers' achievements, songs, poetry, way of life, educational system, prophecies, and even encoded messages on clay pots, stone, and fabrics.

Similarly, we in prison have utilized paños for similar purposes. In the past, paños were employed by inmates to transmit encoded messages from prison to the streets, express love for their families, recount and document their war stories, and even depict their dreams for the future.

The paño art within the prison has played a significant role in preserving our Chicano culture within these confines. As a young individual, I was fortunate enough to learn about the rich history of paño art from one of the elder members of our community. Today, I pass on this knowledge to others, enabling them to navigate through the complexities and challenges of our culture.

Inmate Artist: Solo

My family's roots trace back to East Los Angeles during the 1950s. During that time, all three of my uncles served time in prison. Tio Pelon, in particular, was sentenced to ten years in prison. Despite their troubled past, all three of my uncles possessed immense artistic talent. The Chicano cultural art movement was already thriving in California during that era, with numerous murals adorning the walls of East Los Angeles, depicting our rich heritage.

Within the confines of my uncles' rooms and the garage, one could find an abundance of meticulously crafted paños, neatly hung with great care. These paños were painstakingly created using blue or black ink and often required a minimum of 60 hours to complete. They featured various elements such as the Mexican flag, eagles, jaguars, muscular homies, lowriders, and an array of captivating hynas. As a young boy, I was particularly drawn to the paños that showcased beautiful ladies.

My uncles had two strict rules when it came to their cherished paños. Firstly, they were never to be exposed to direct sunlight, as the ink and markers used could fade over time. Secondly, no one was allowed to touch these prized possessions. Any violation of this rule would result in a spanking, as it could potentially damage the delicate artwork.

Although the exact origins of Mexica art on paños in Califas remain unclear, it gained significant popularity in East Los Angeles during the 1950s. When tio Pelon passed away in 1978, he was laid to rest alongside all of his beloved paños. Tio Bucky, on the other hand, transitioned his artistic skills from paños to creating business signs throughout the city of Montebello.

Inmate Artist: Dreamer

Art has been a source of immense support for me, particularly during the most challenging times in my life. Following my involvement in a crime, I was well aware that I would be confined to a prison cell for an extended period. While I acknowledged my responsibility, I couldn't escape the overwhelming emotions of fear, anger, and loneliness. However, through drawing, I found solace and a means to liberate my mind from the confines of my small cell, where sunlight was a rarity and communication with loved ones was severely restricted. Family and friends were only permitted to visit for a mere 30 minutes on Fridays, Saturdays, and Sundays. I held onto the hope that my parents would somehow secure my release, but as time passed, I sank deeper into depression without expressing or revealing it. Art became my refuge, consuming six to eight hours of my day. Initially, it served as a form of meditation, but gradually transformed into a means of survival.

I would draw for pastries and chocolate bars; to me, those were luxuries. My family sent me money to buy what I needed, not what I wanted. Today, I still hustle my drawing because it's a way to help my family. Although it may not be sufficient to cover household expenses, it does alleviate the burden of their expenditure on my packages or canteen. I am constantly striving to improve my skills, and I am grateful to God for blessing me with this talent, which serves as an ongoing journey of learning and growth.

Paños

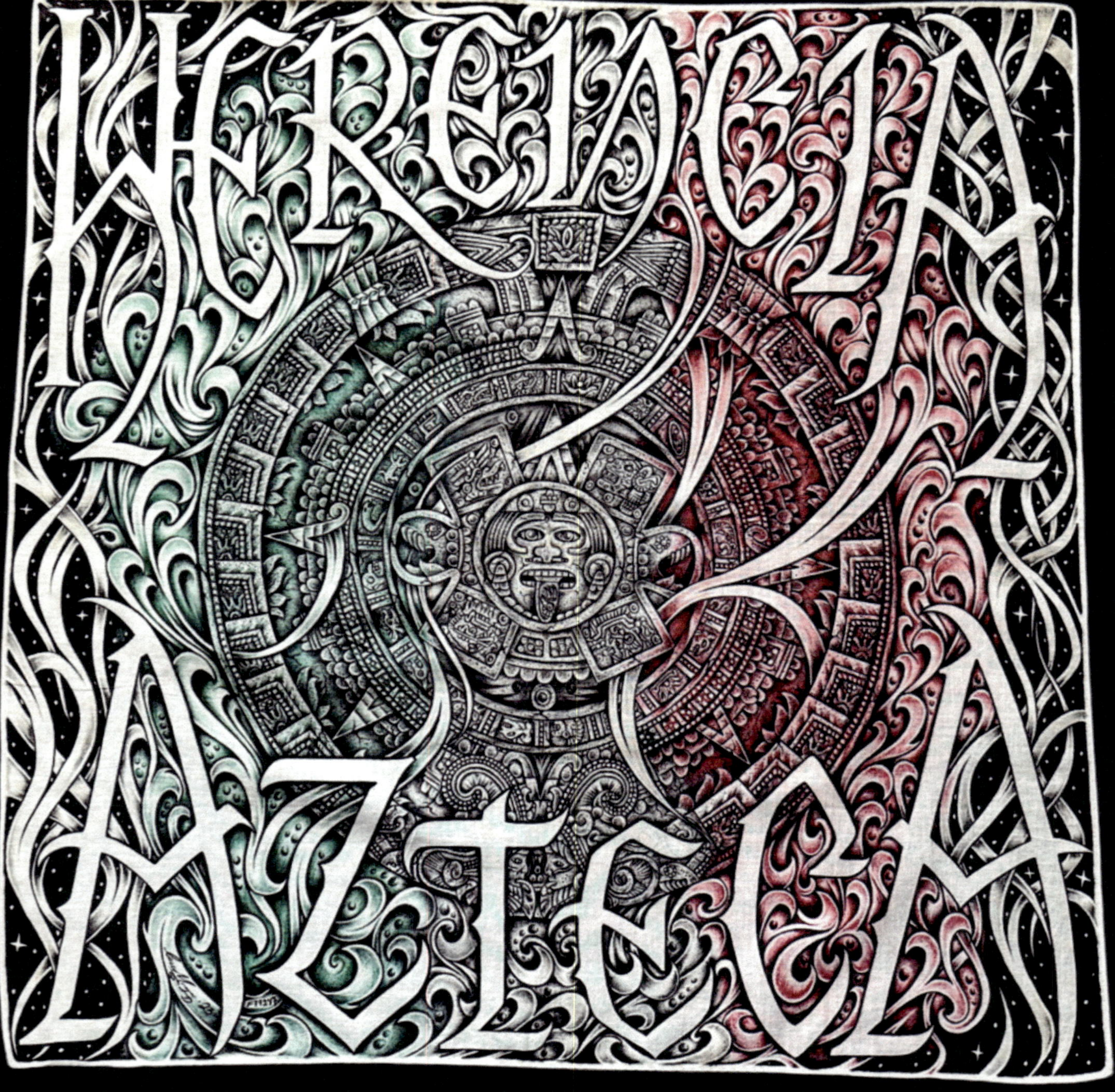
HERENCIA
AZTECA

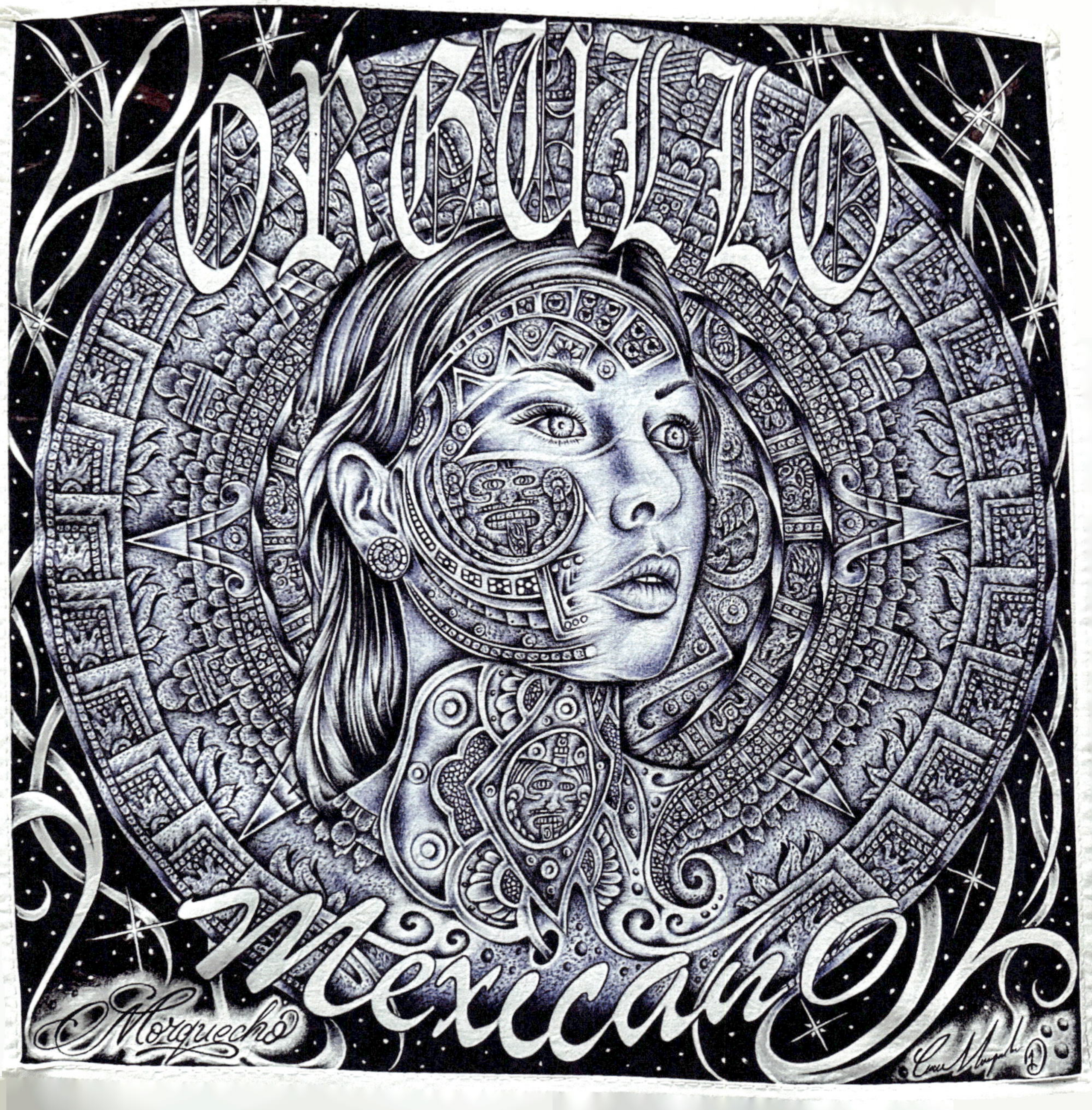
ORGULLO
Mexicano
Morquecho

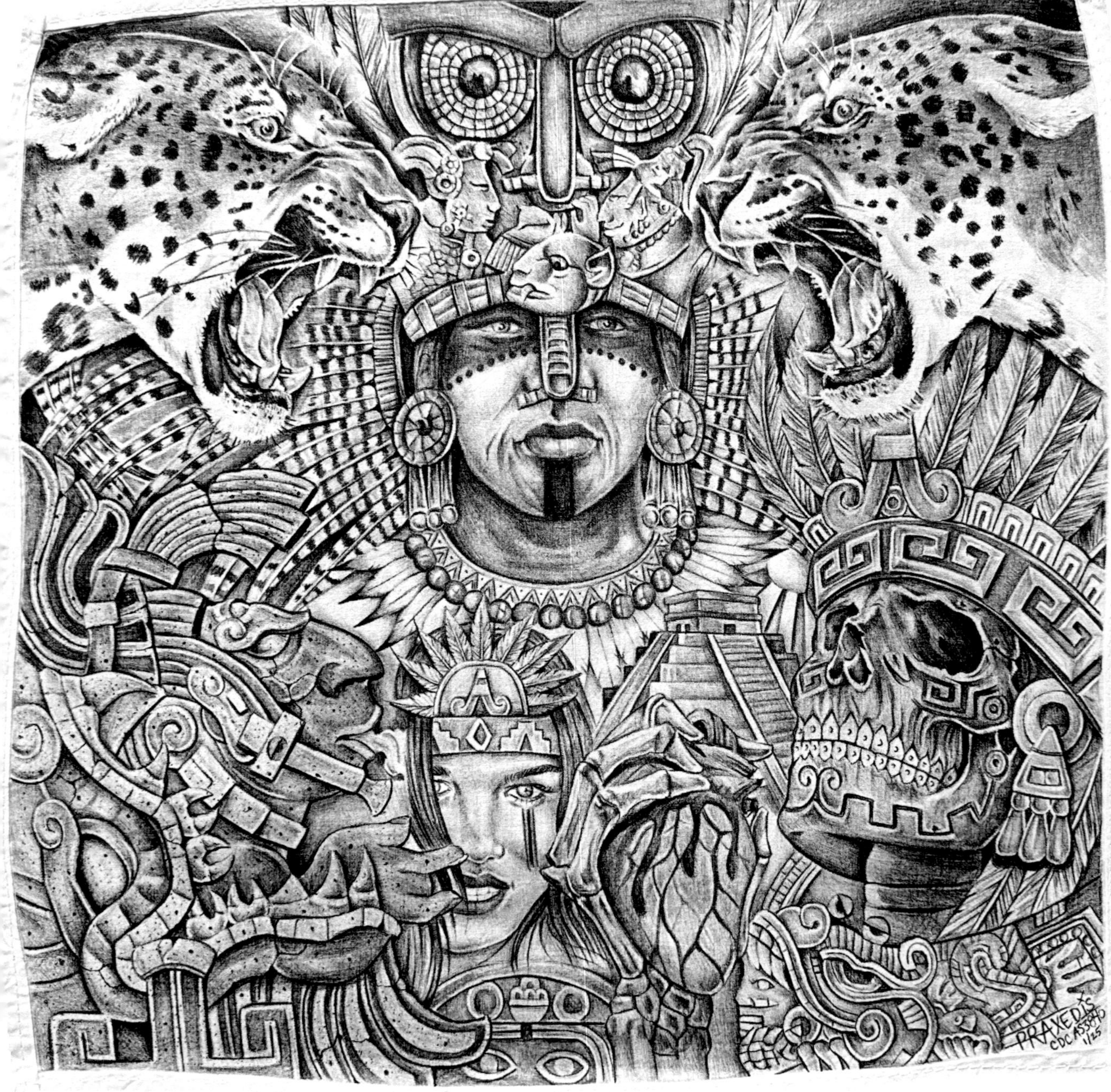
PRAXEDIS
1/25

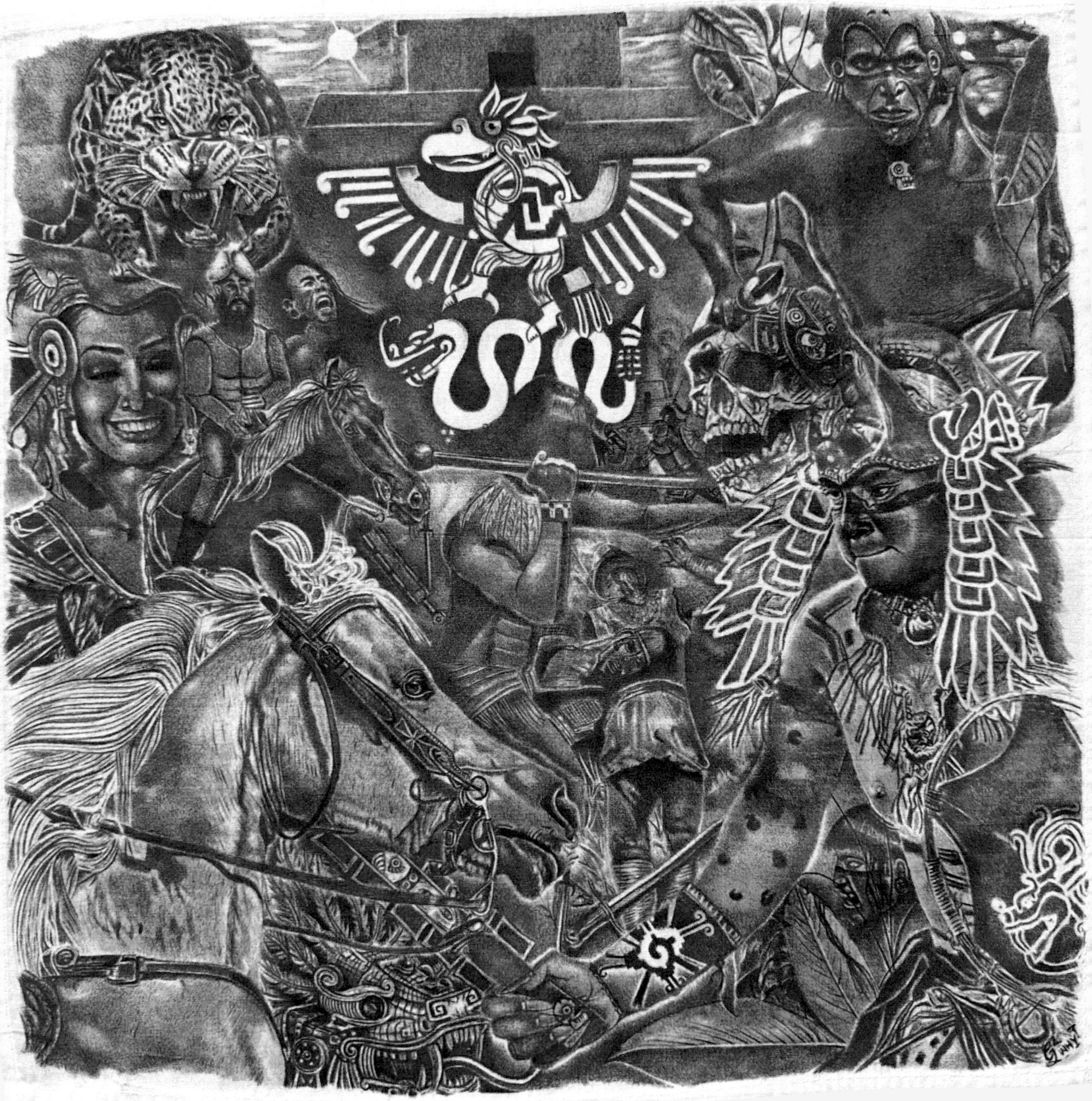

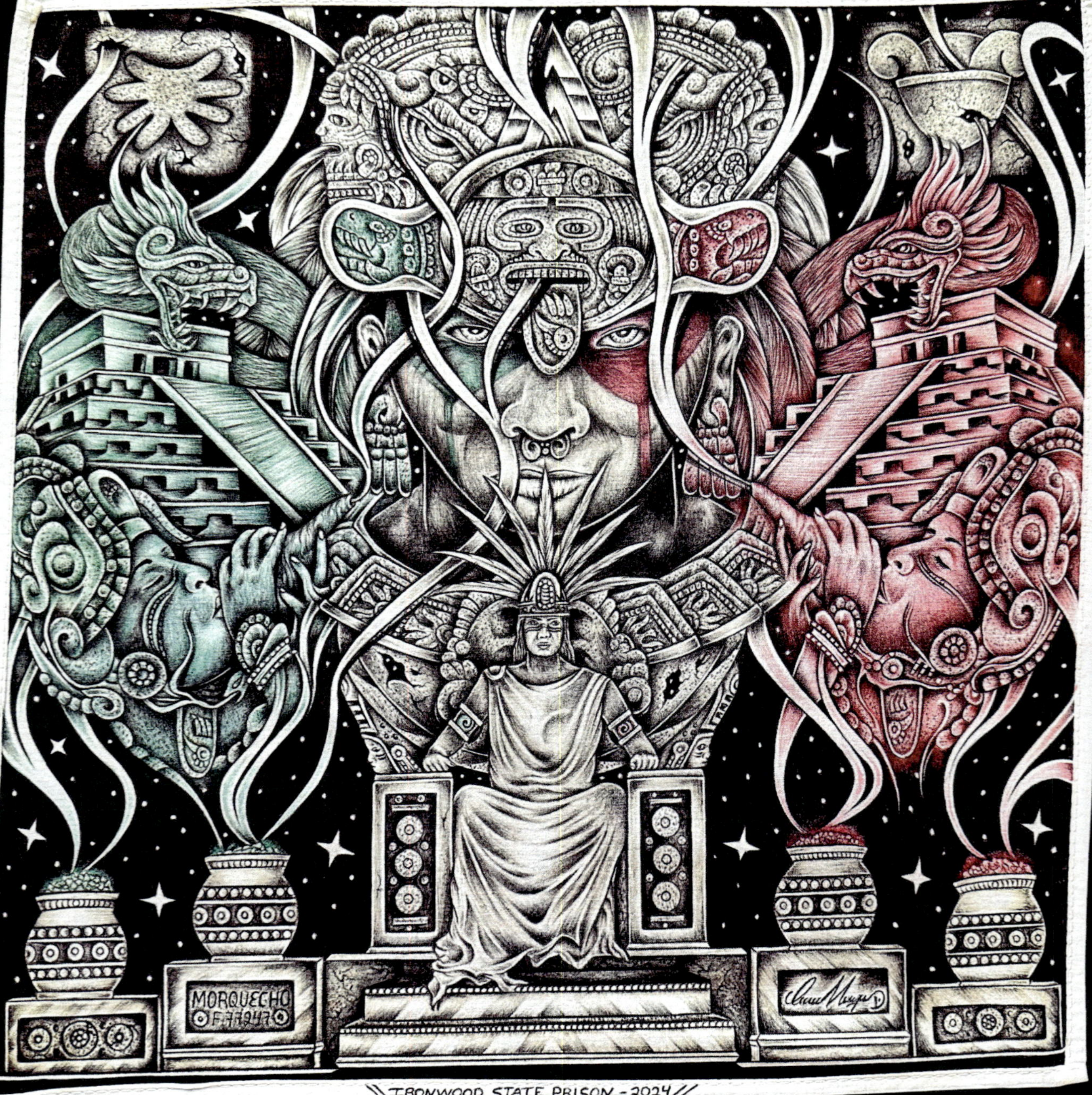

IRONWOOD STATE PRISON - 2024

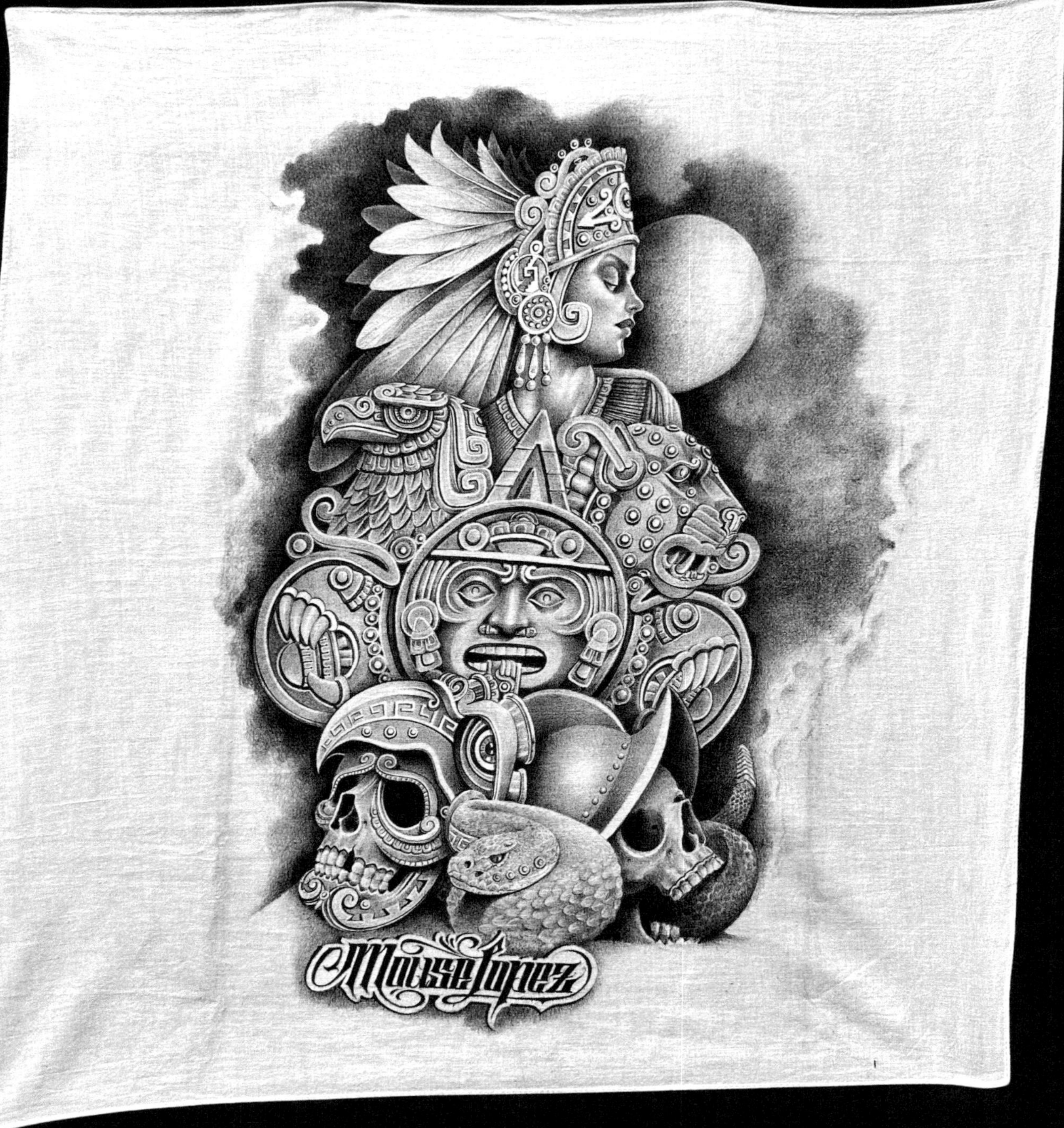
MouseLopez

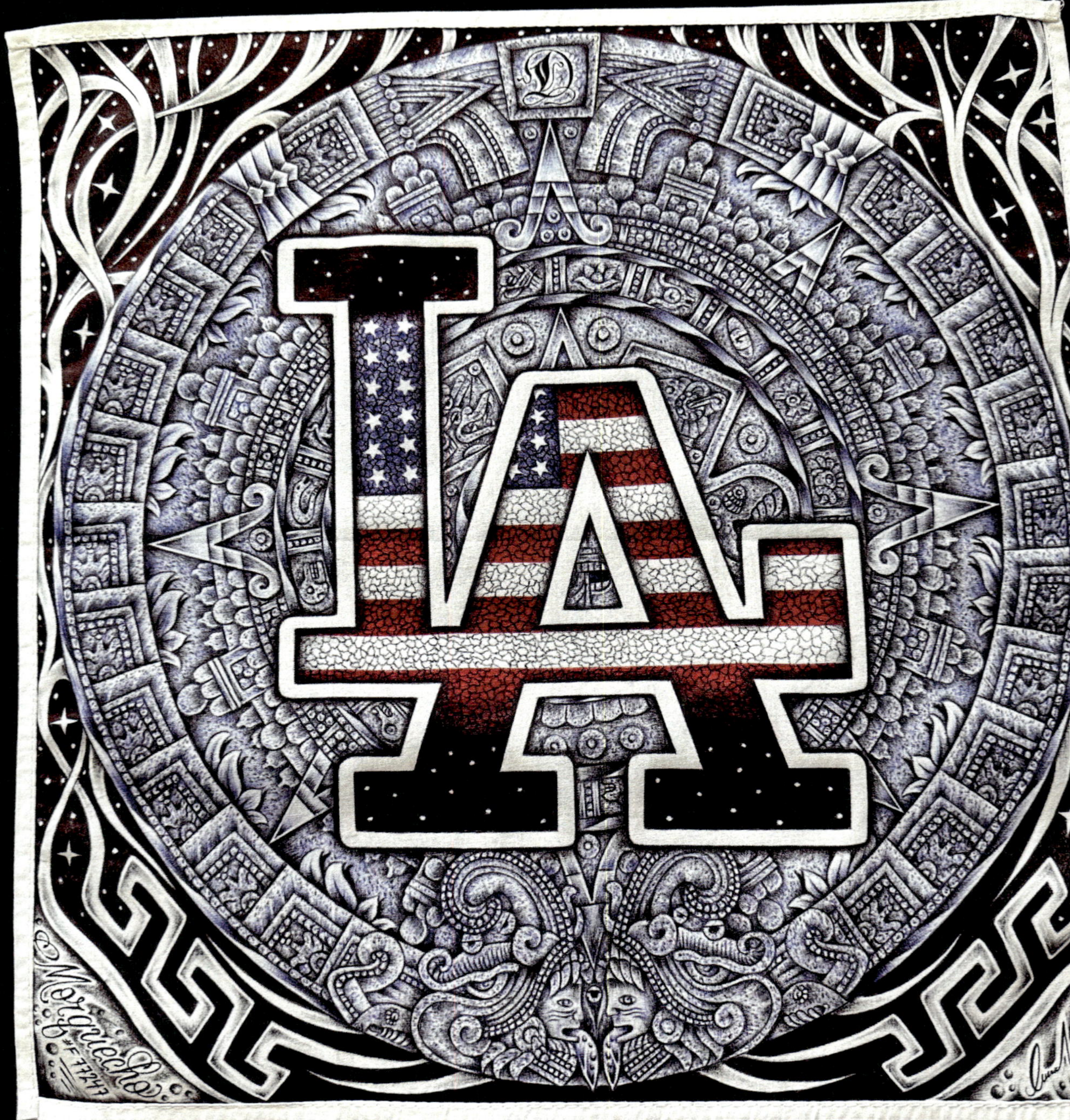
LA
Morguecho
#F77247

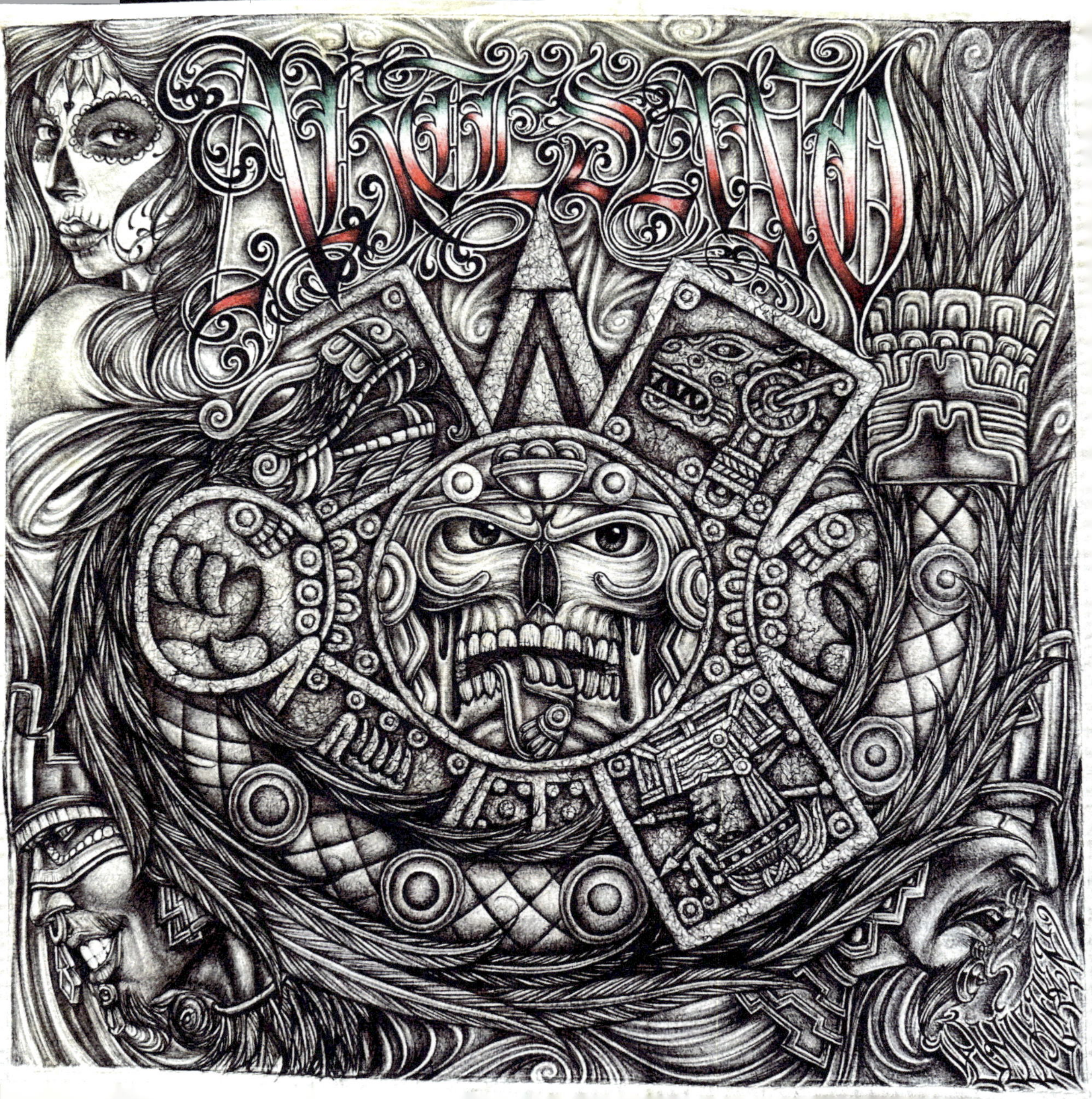

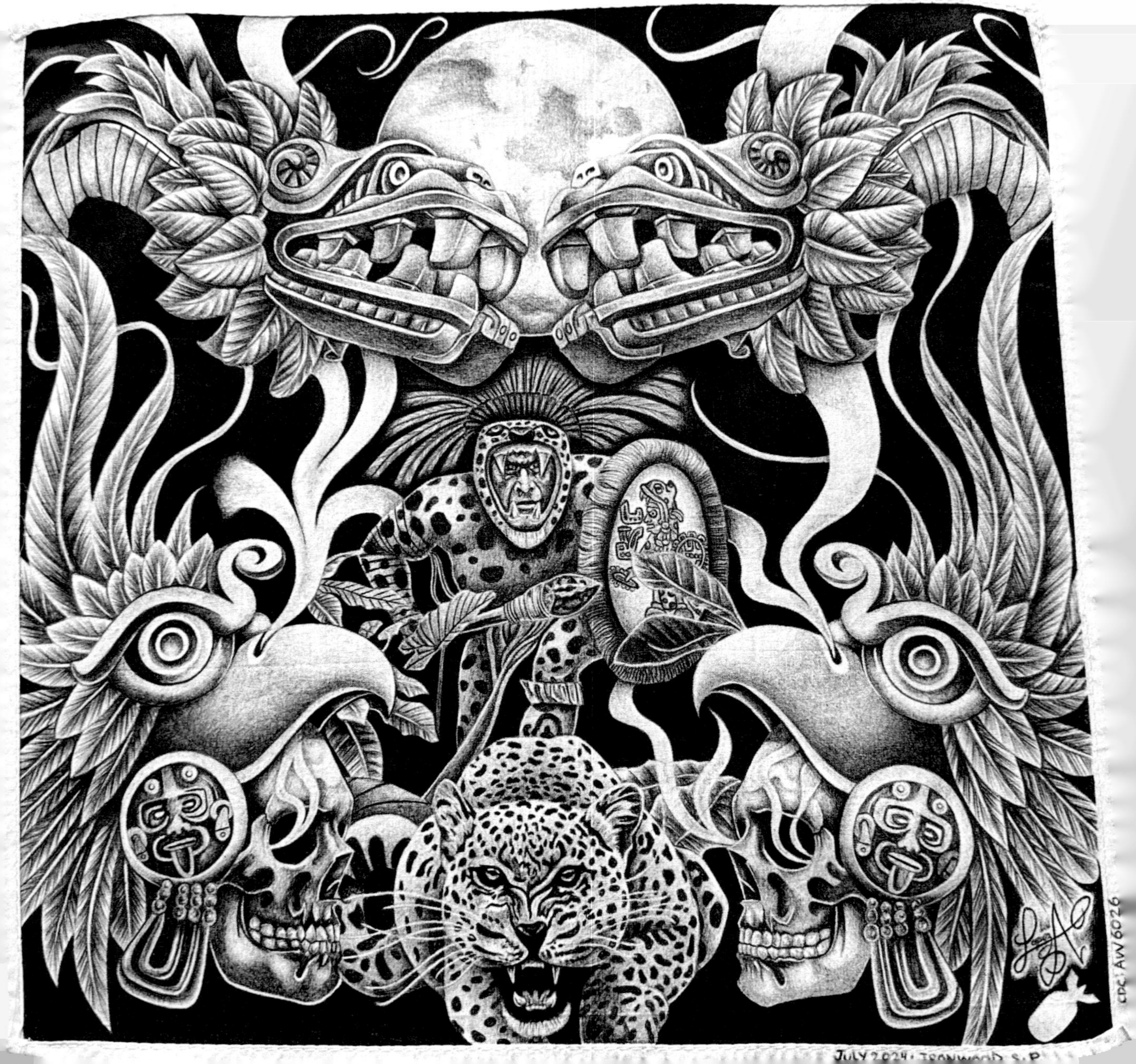
CDC: AW6026
JULY 2024 · IRONWOOD S.P

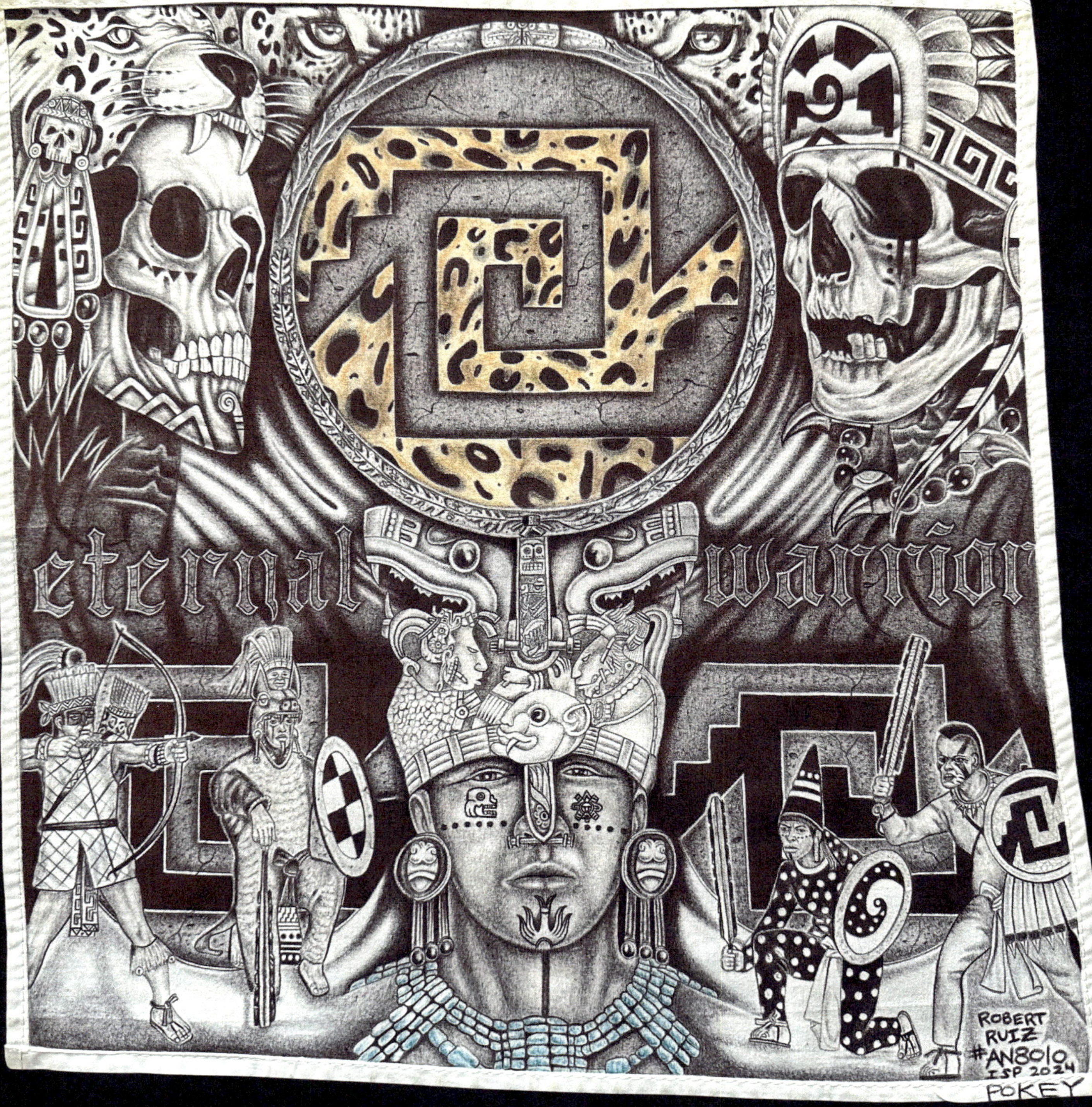
eternal
warrior
ROBERT
RUIZ
#AN8010
ISP 2024
POKEY

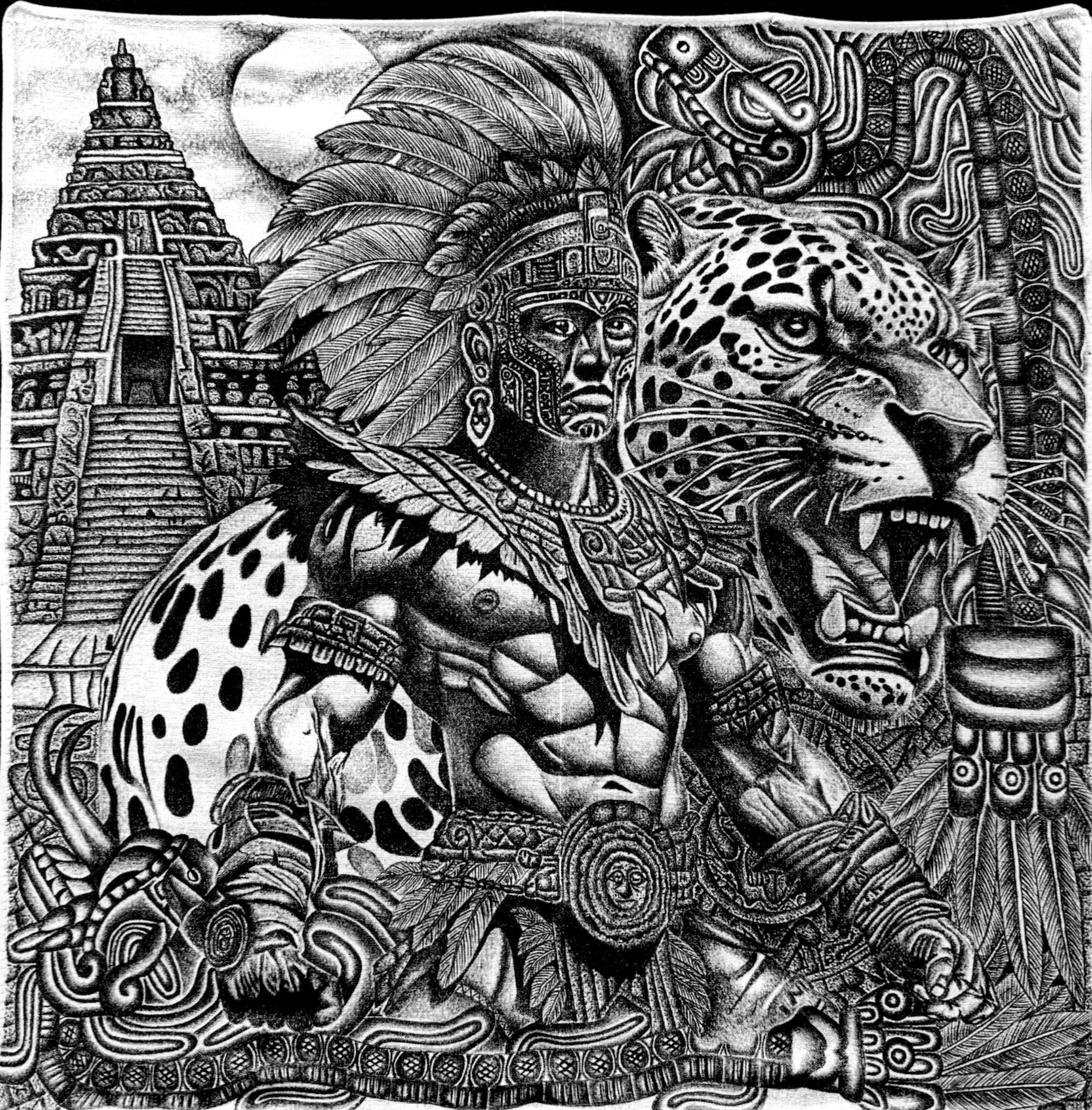

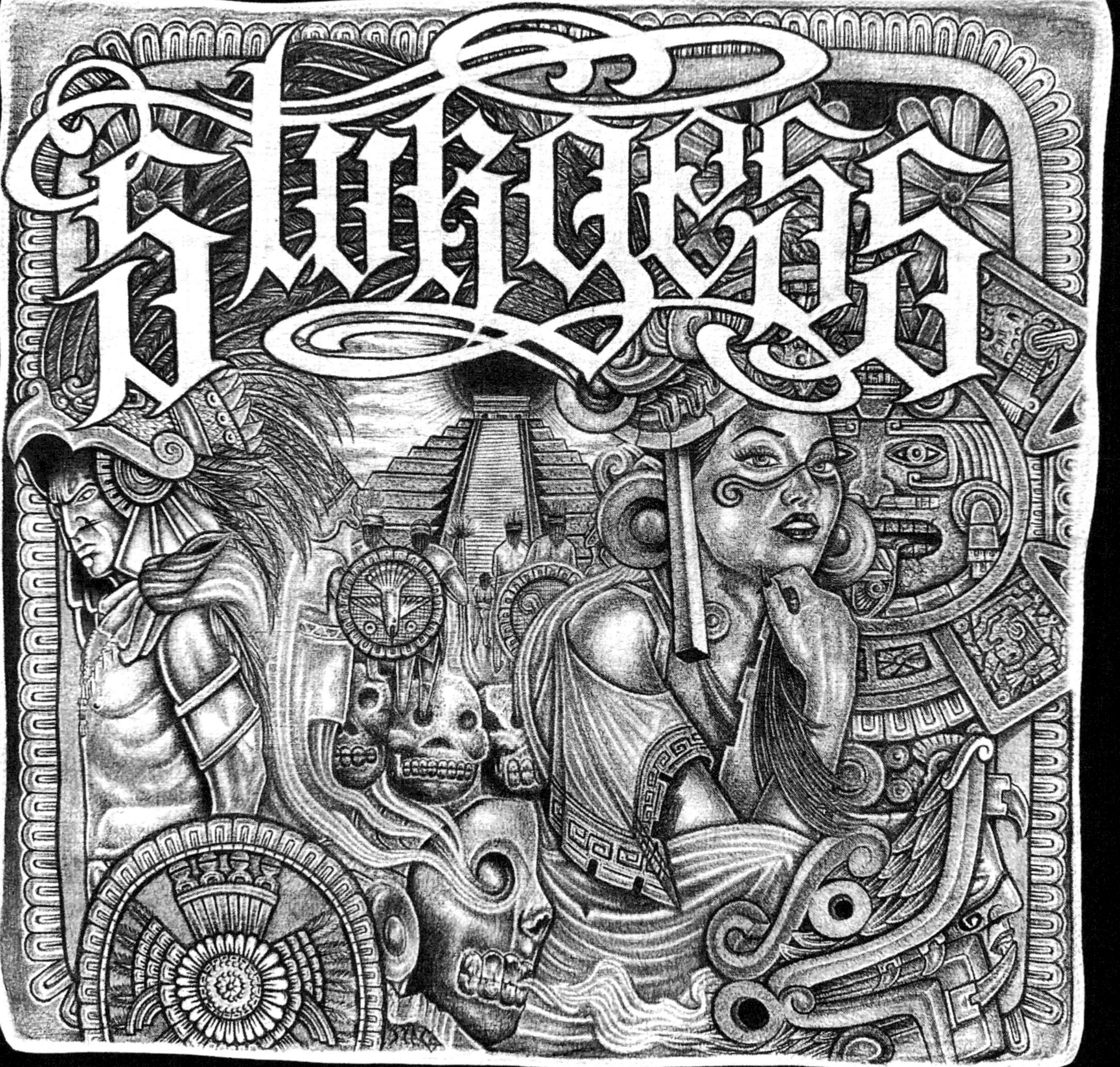

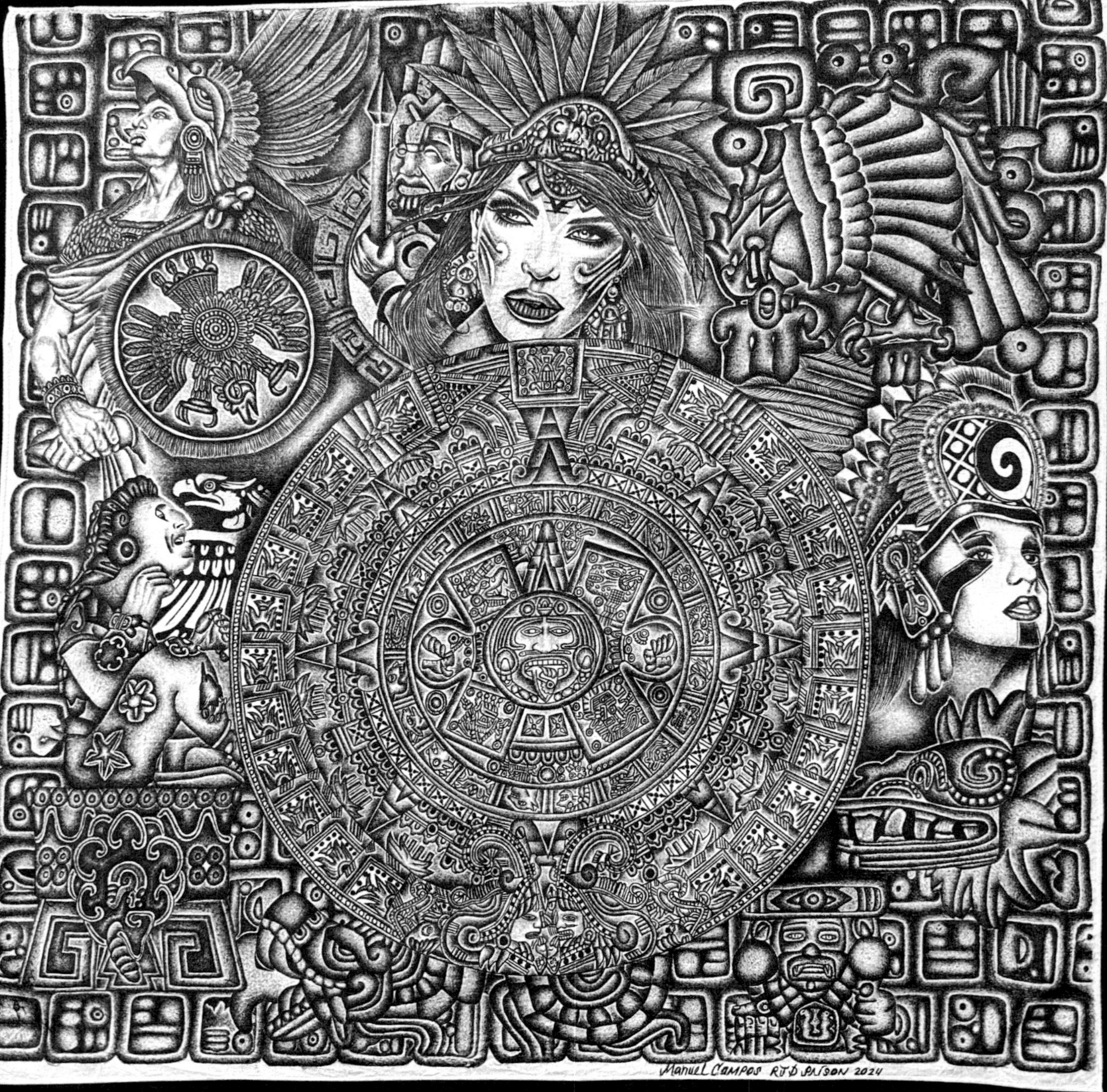
Manuel Campos RJD Prison 2024

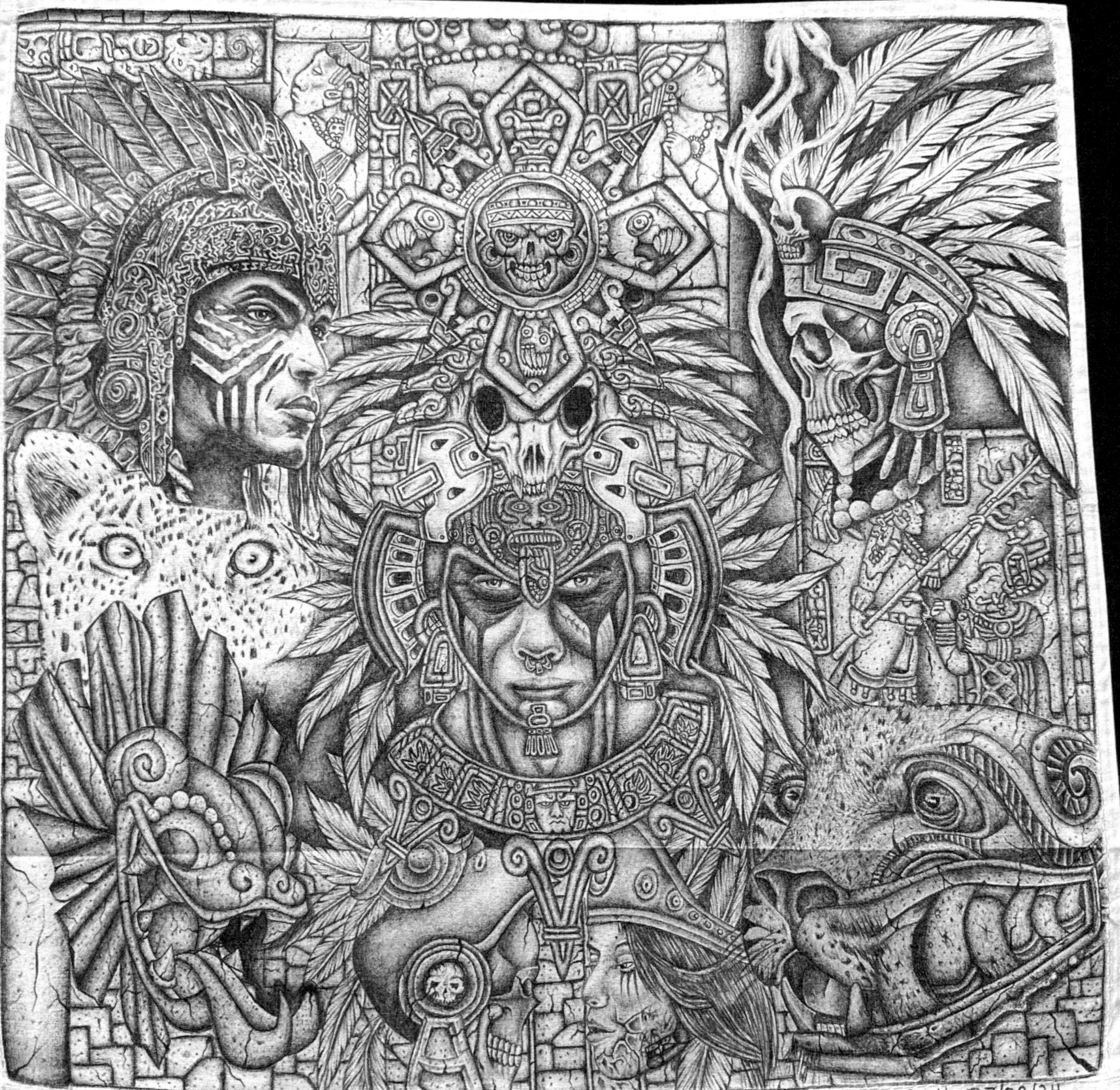

BR9232 William Esparza IRONWOOD STATE PRISON 03/02/24

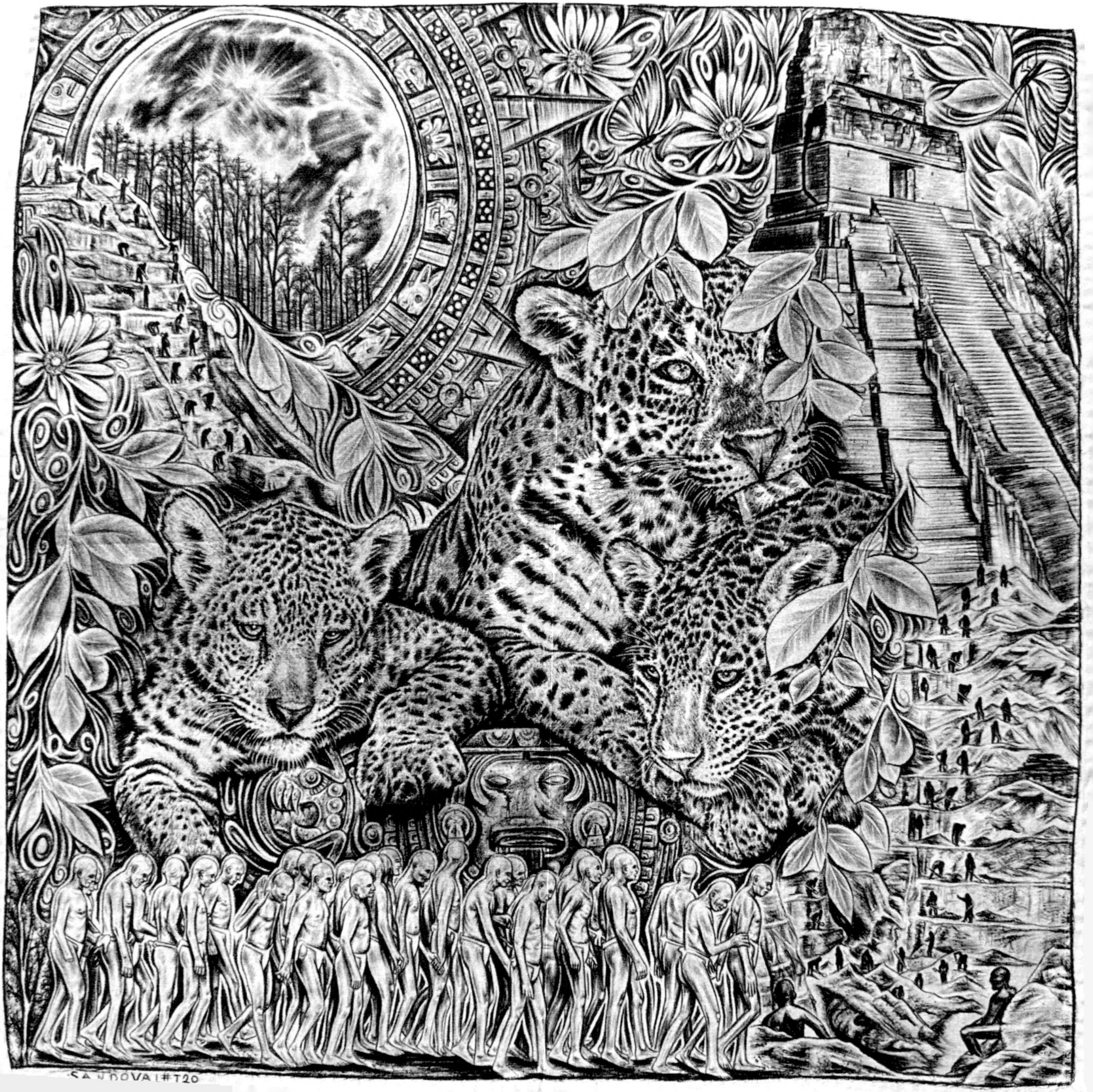
SANDOVAL#T20

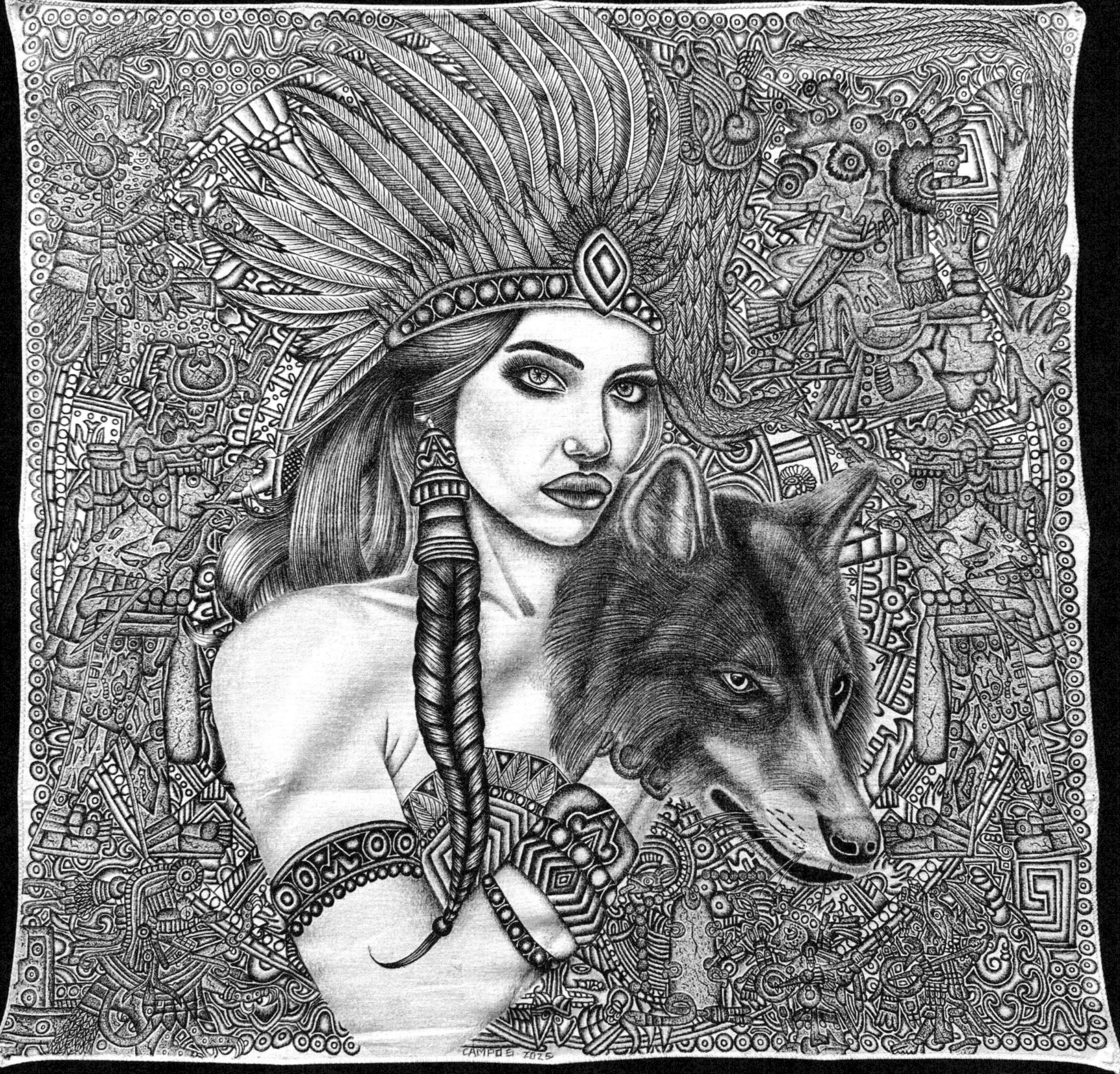
CAMPOS 2025

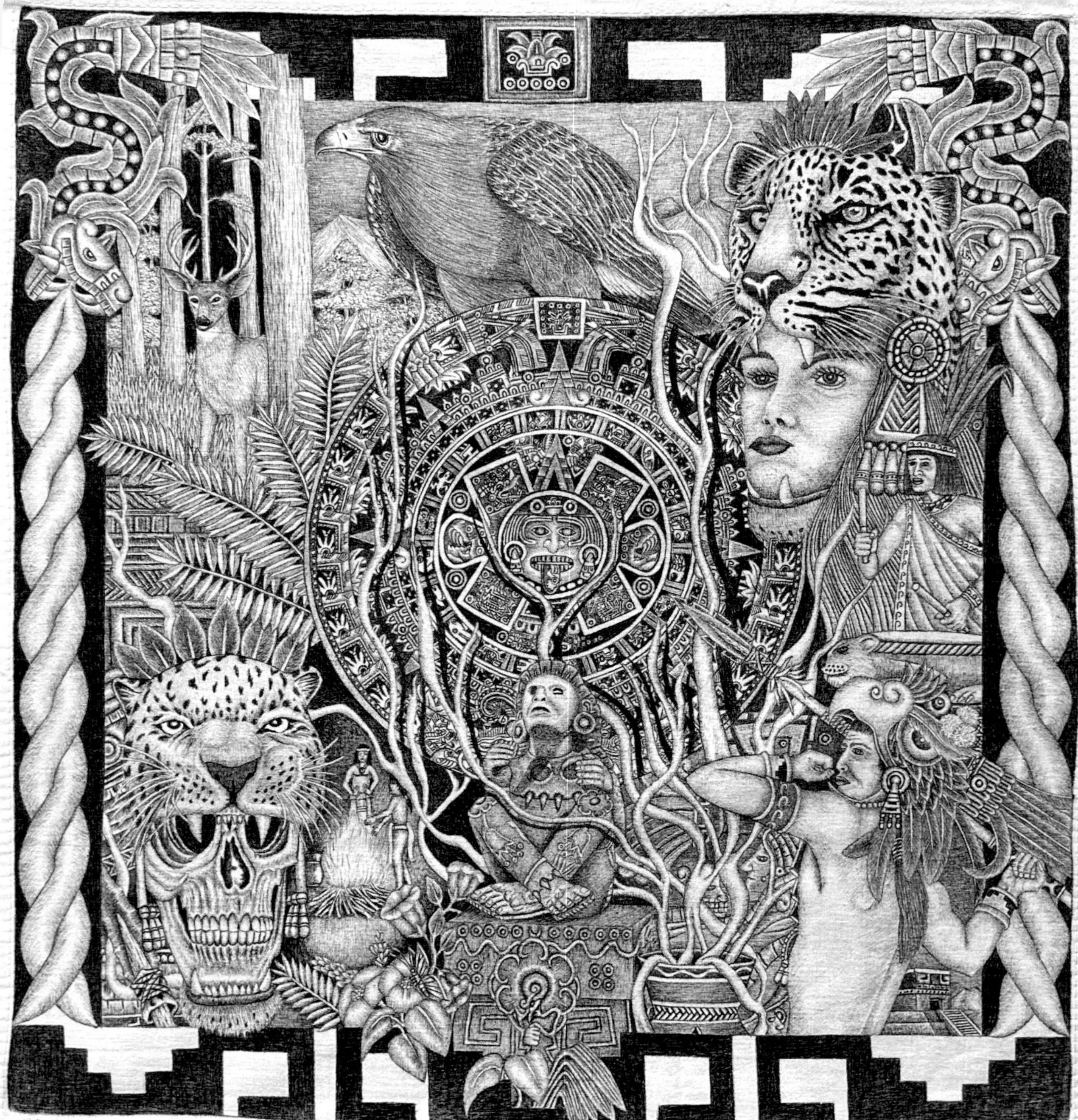

IRONWOOD STATE PRISON

ART GEORGE CDC# T-00826 5-5-2024

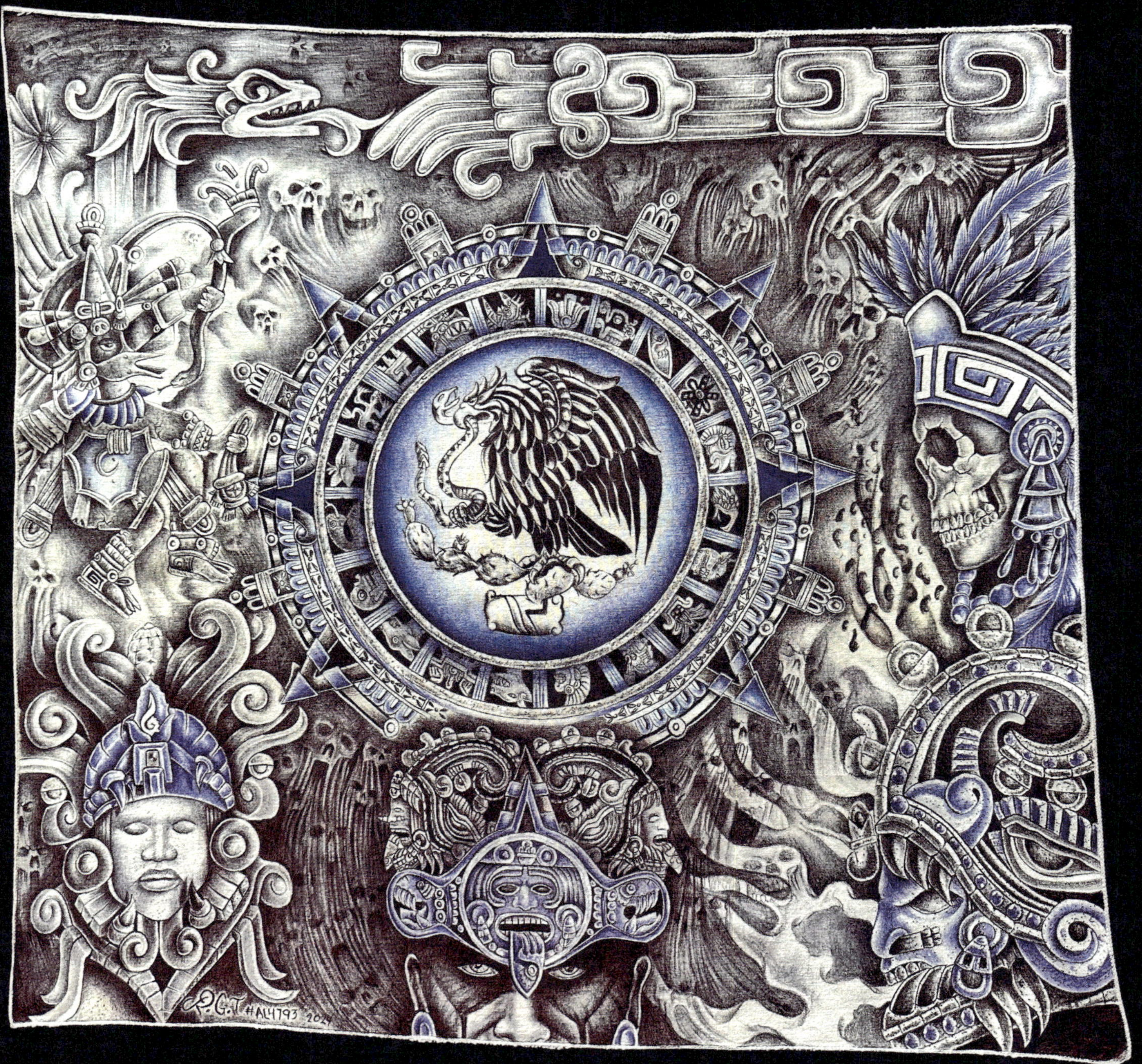
R.G.T #AL4793 2024

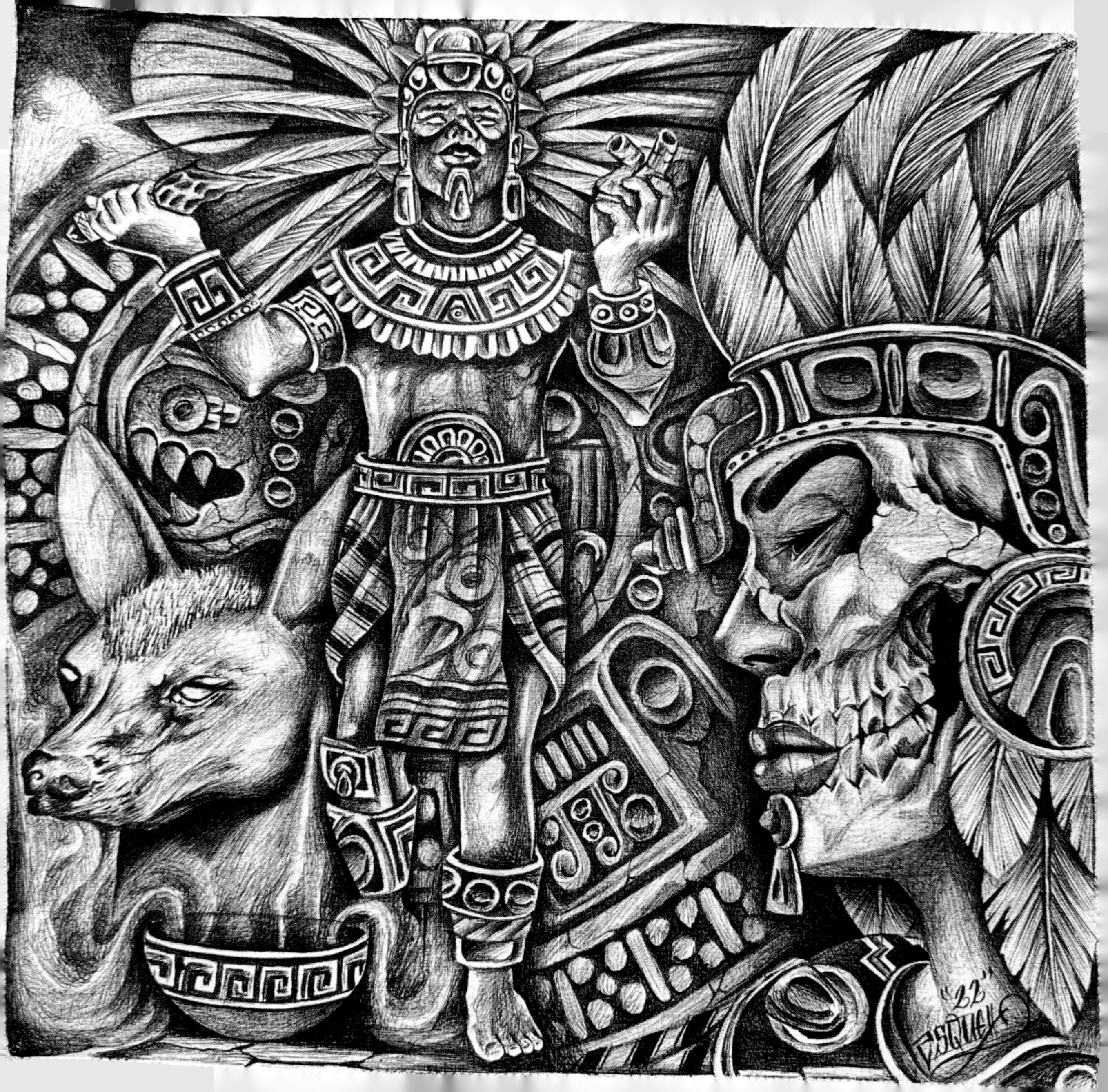
"22"

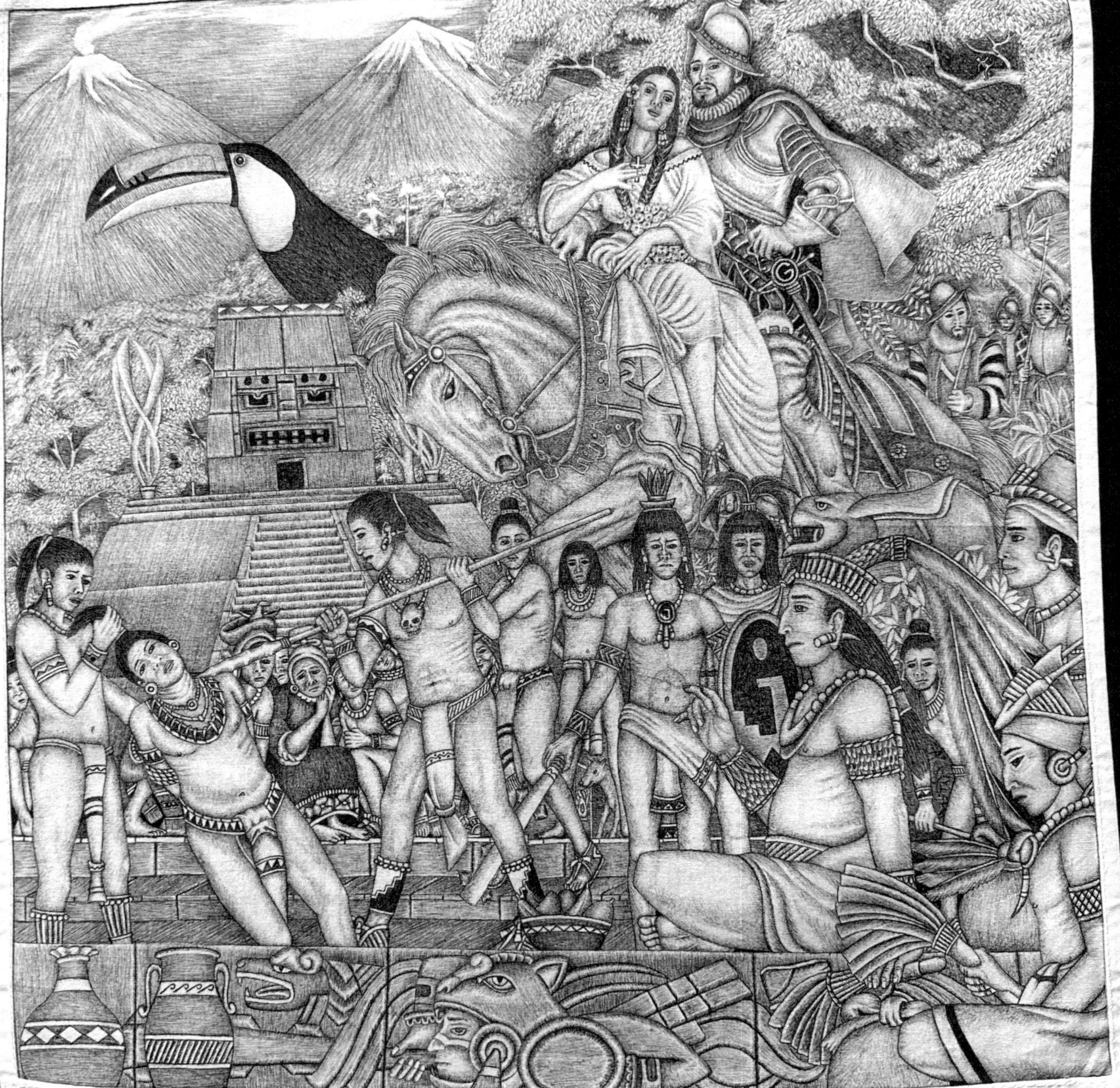

IRONWOOD STATE PRISON 2·4·2024 xART GEORGE CDC T-00826

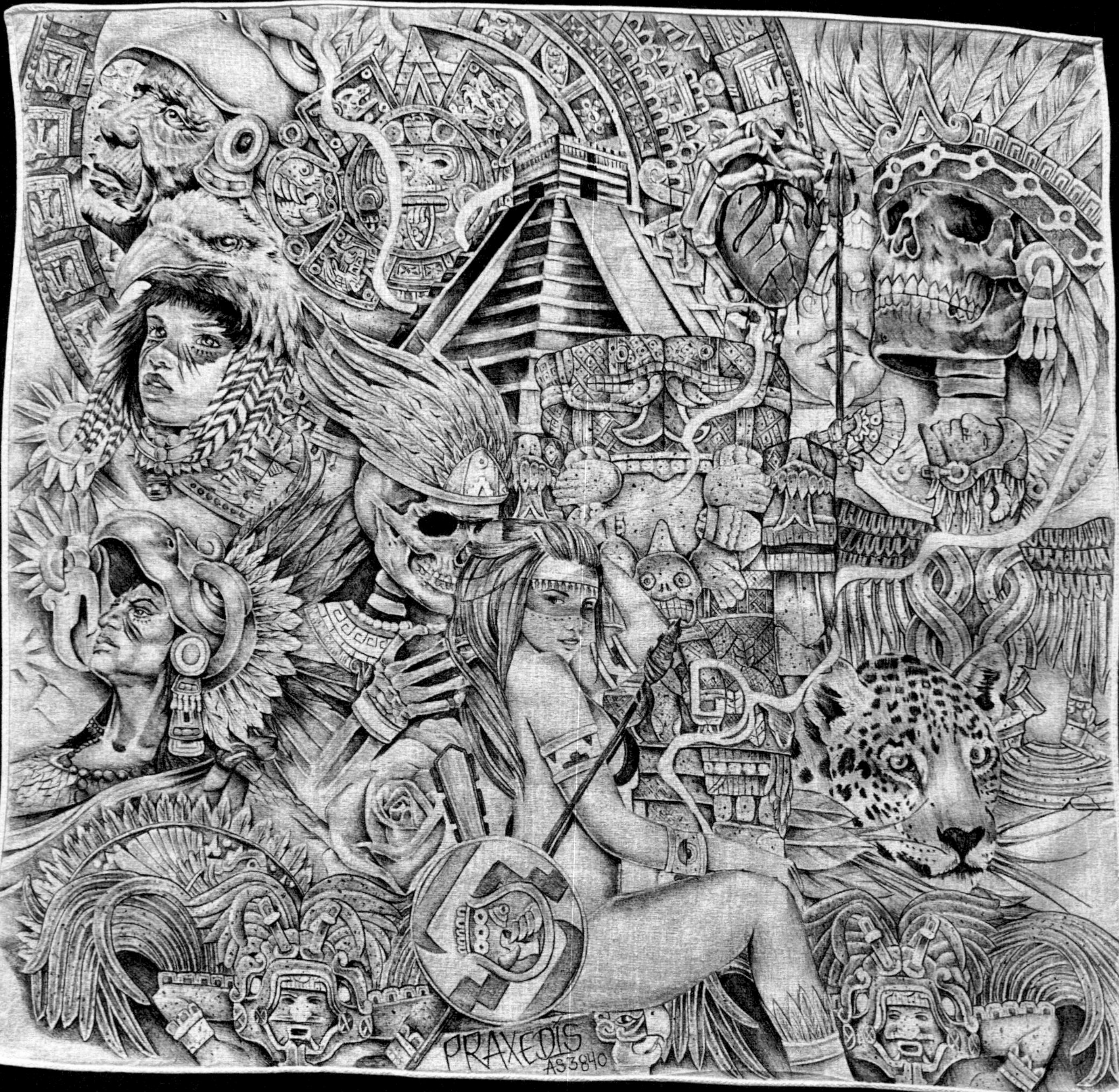
PRAXEDIS
AS3840

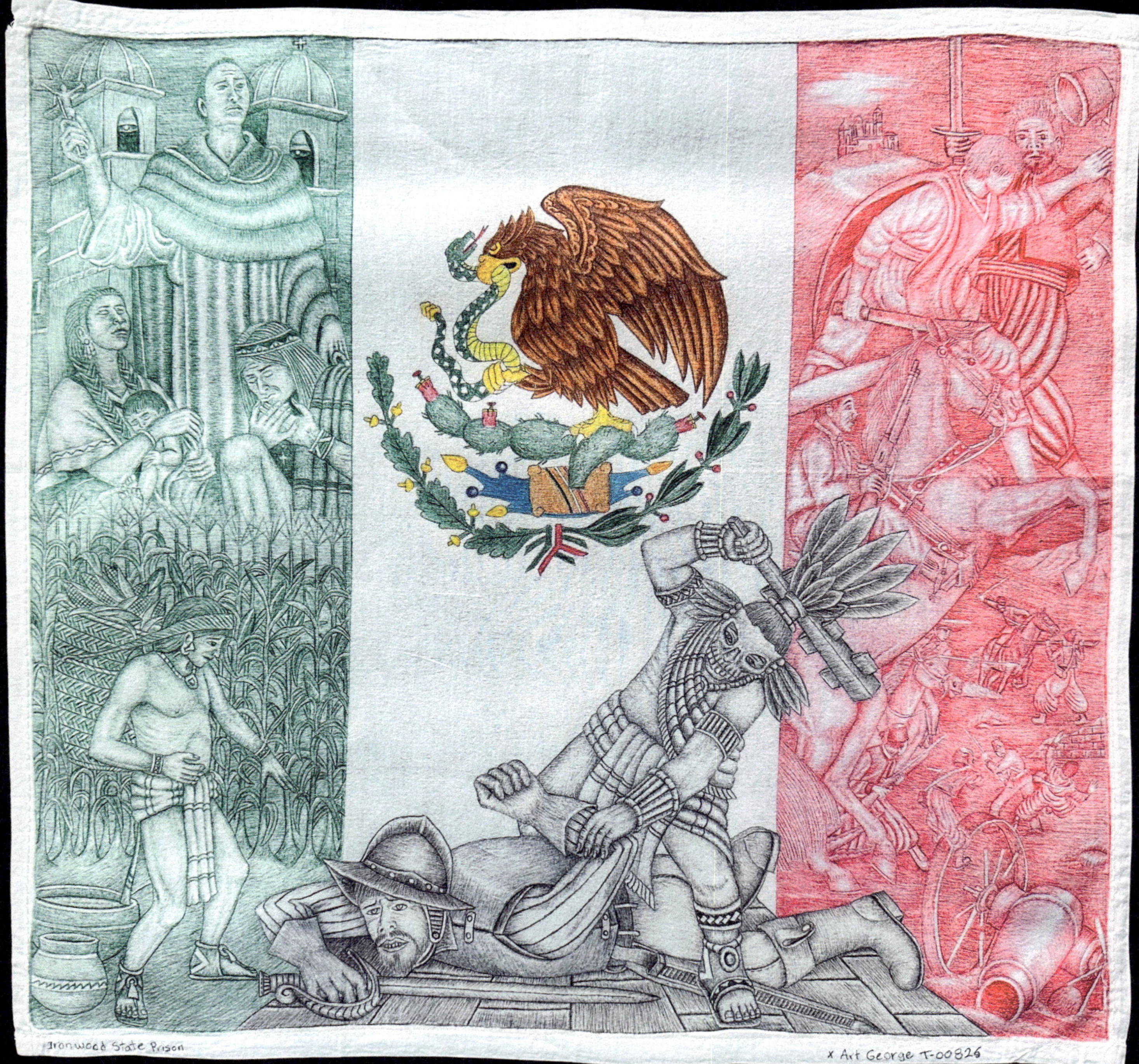
Ironwood State Prison
x Art George T-00826

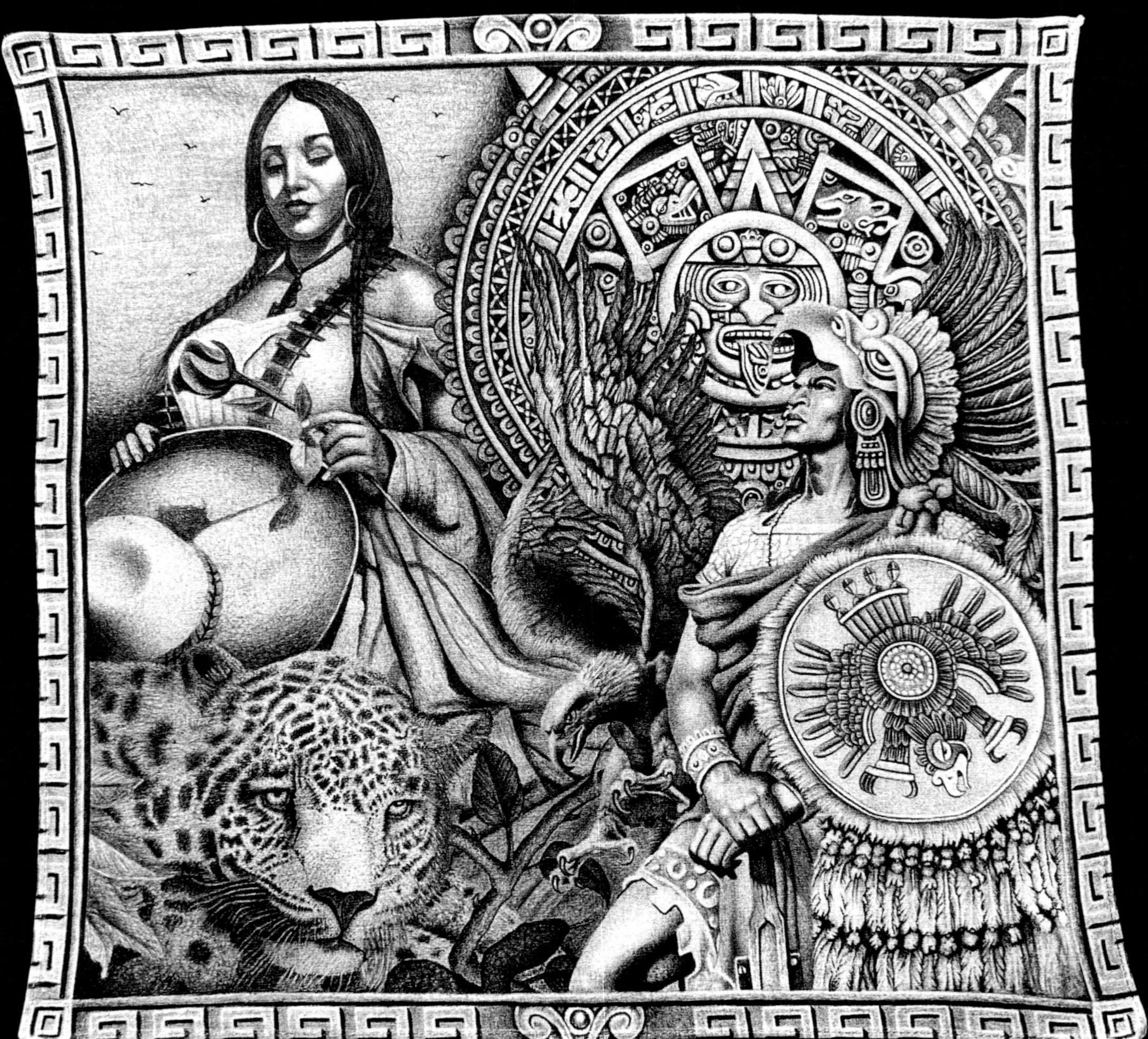

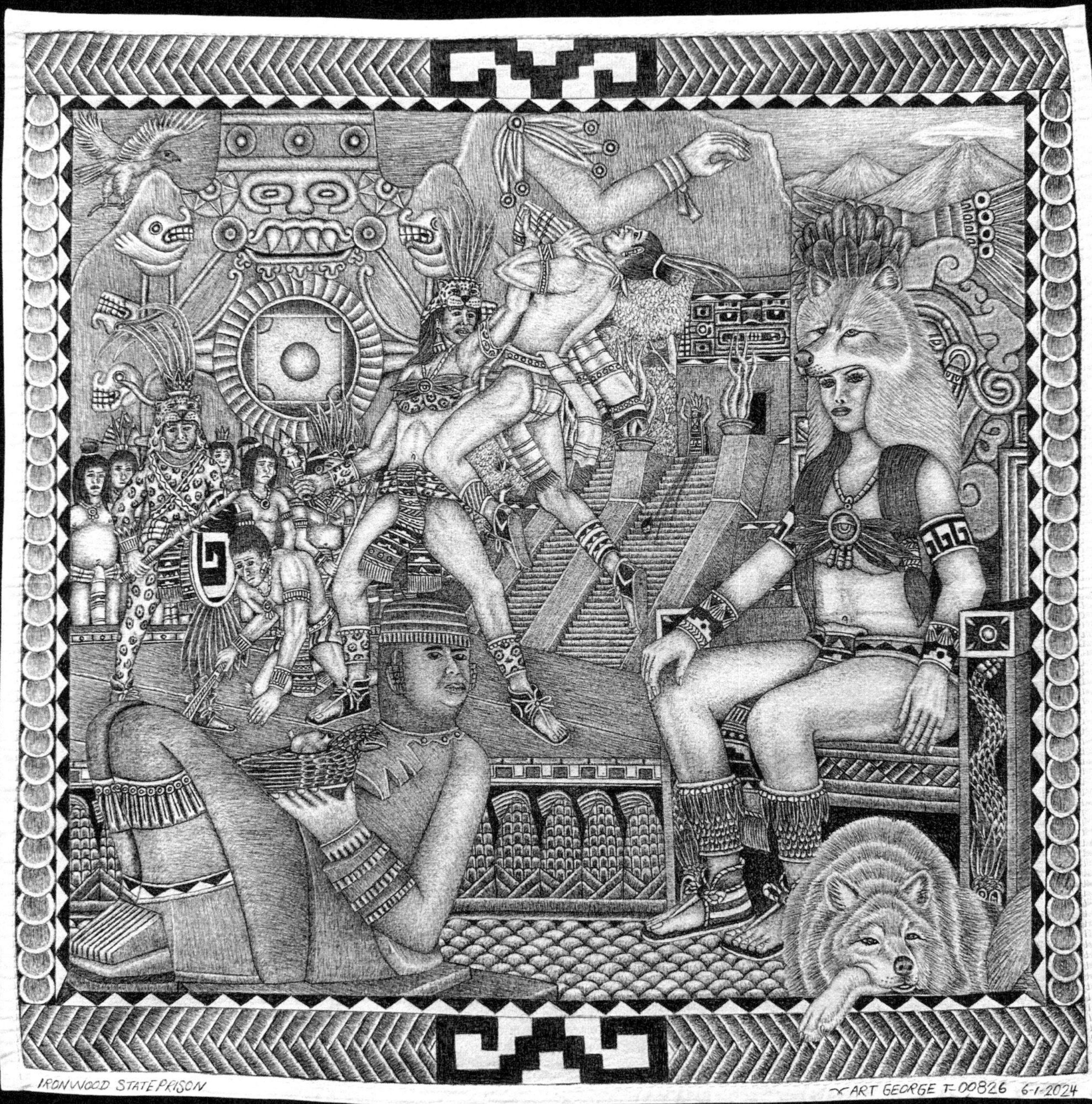
IRONWOOD STATE PRISON
ART GEORGE T-00826 6-1-2024

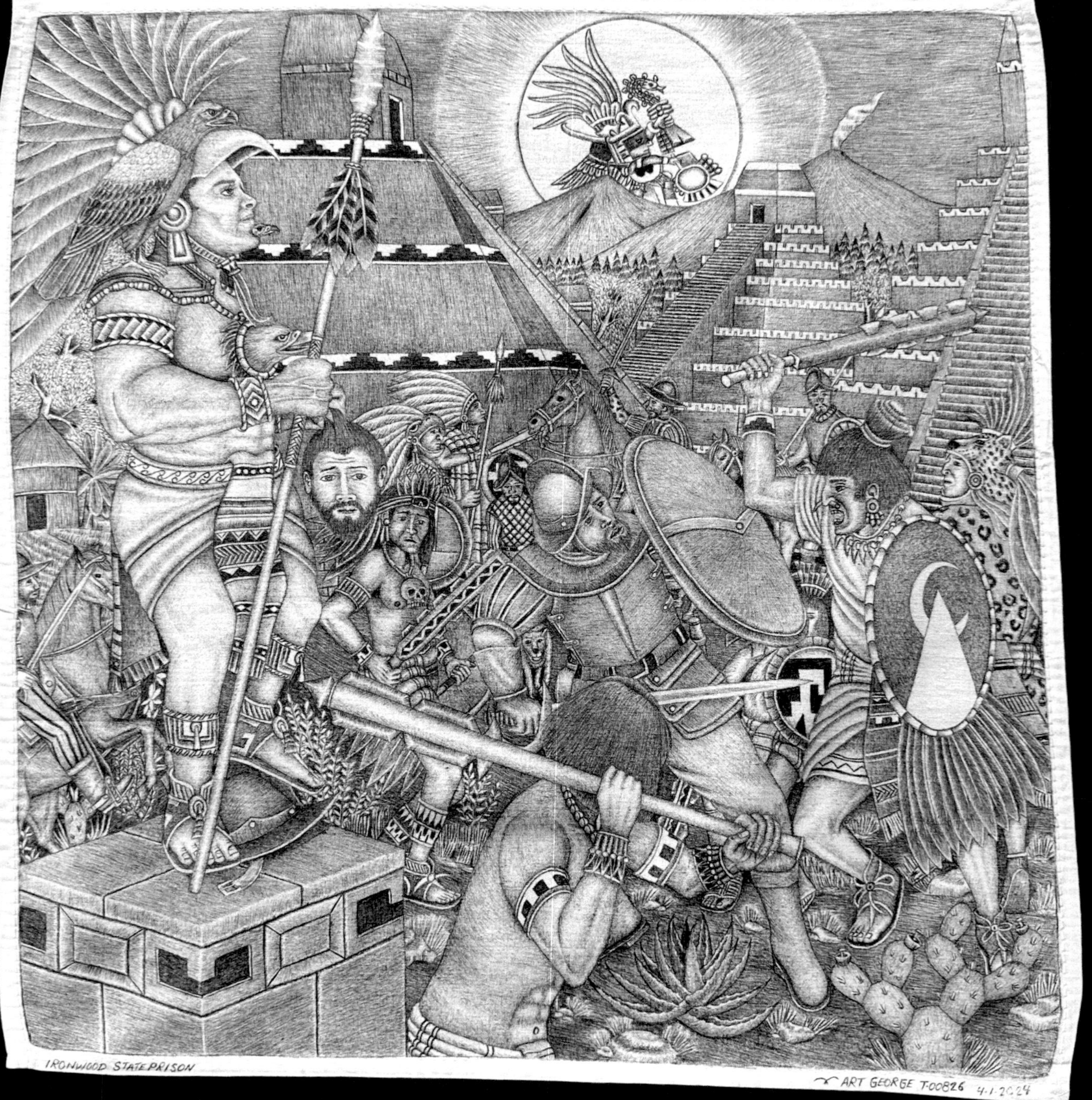
IRONWOOD STATEPRISON
ART GEORGE T-00826 4-1-2024

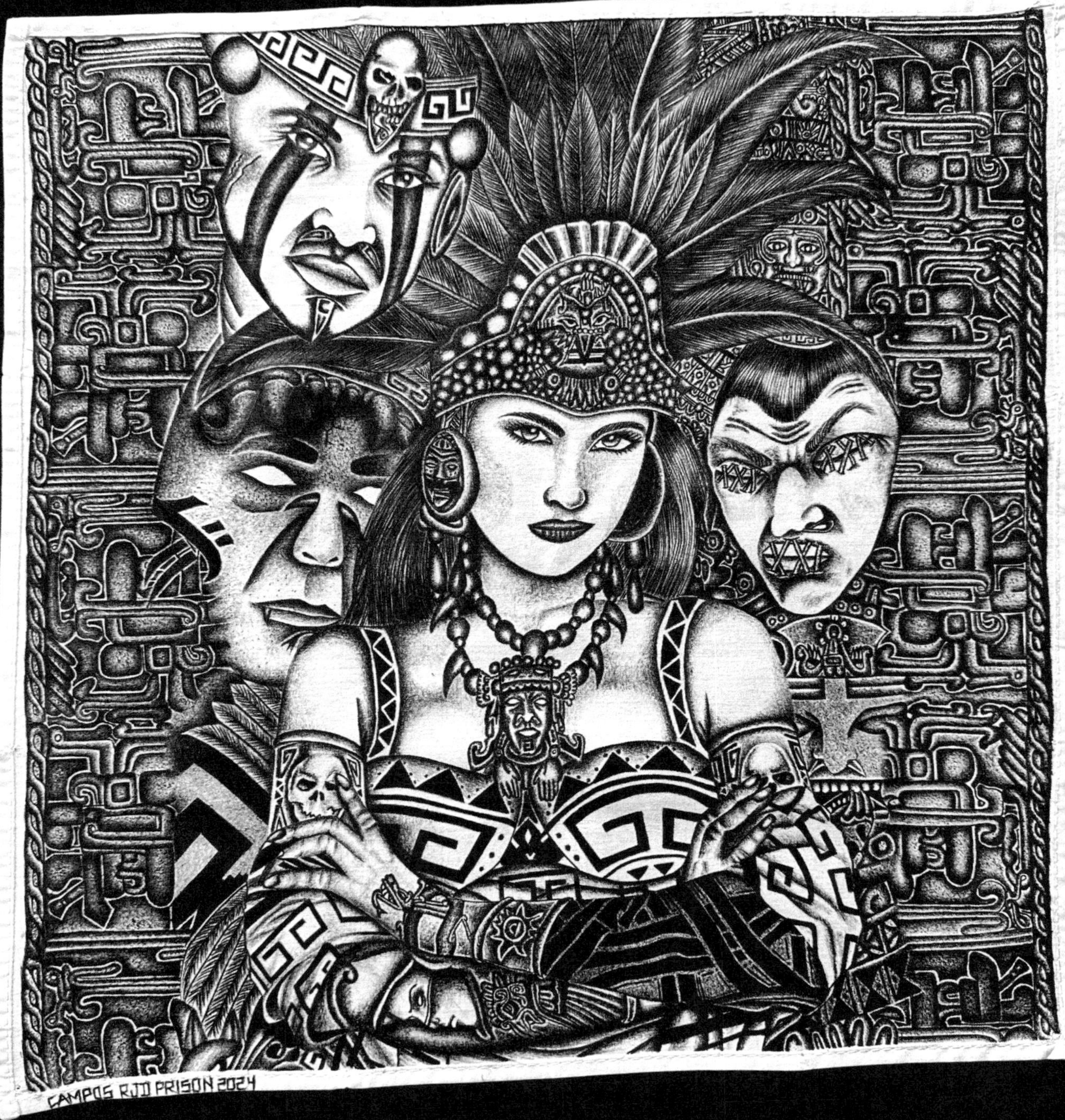
CAMPOS RJD PRISON 2024

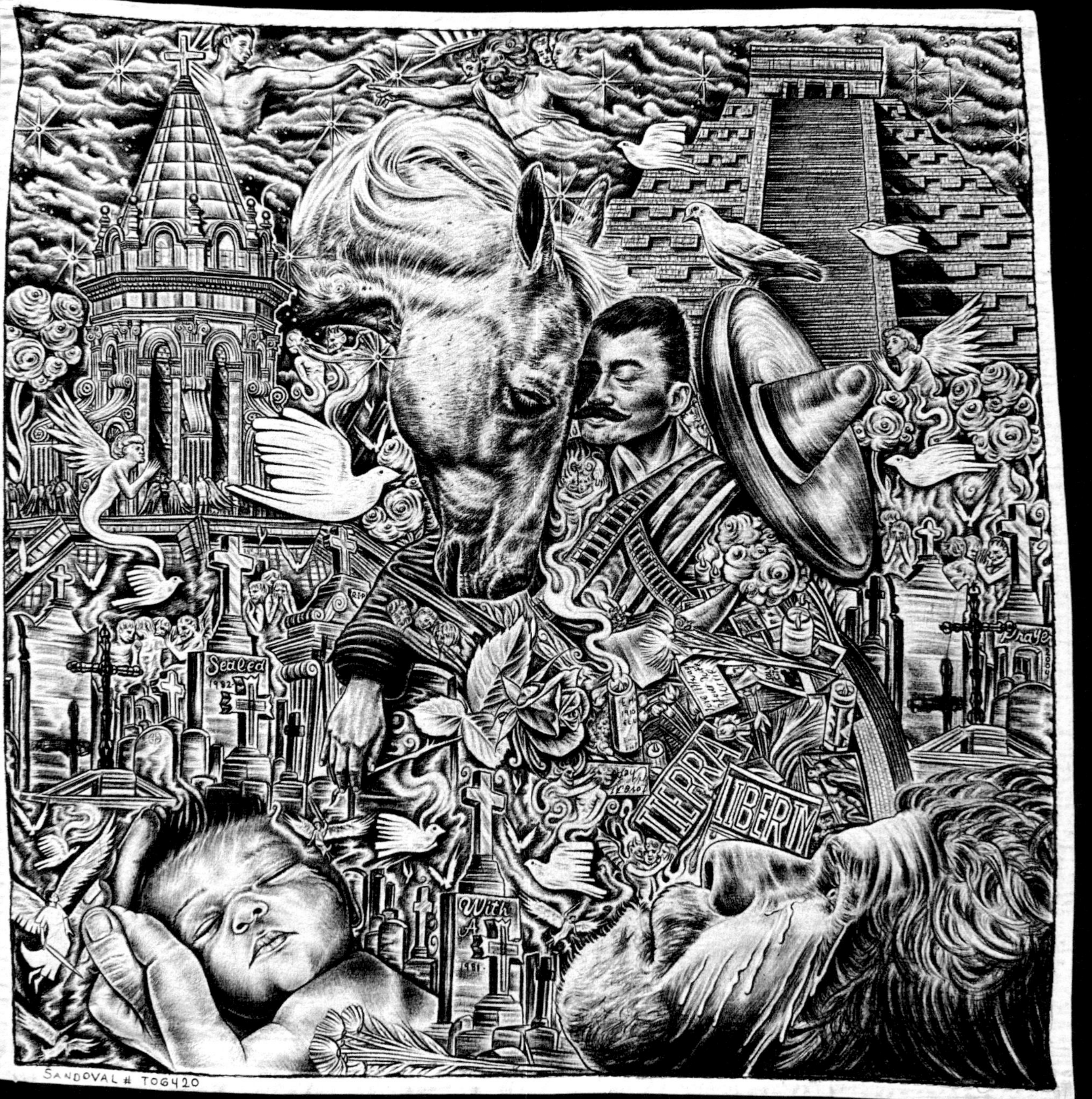
Sealed
TIERRA
LIBERTY
With
Prayer
SANDOVAL # TO6420

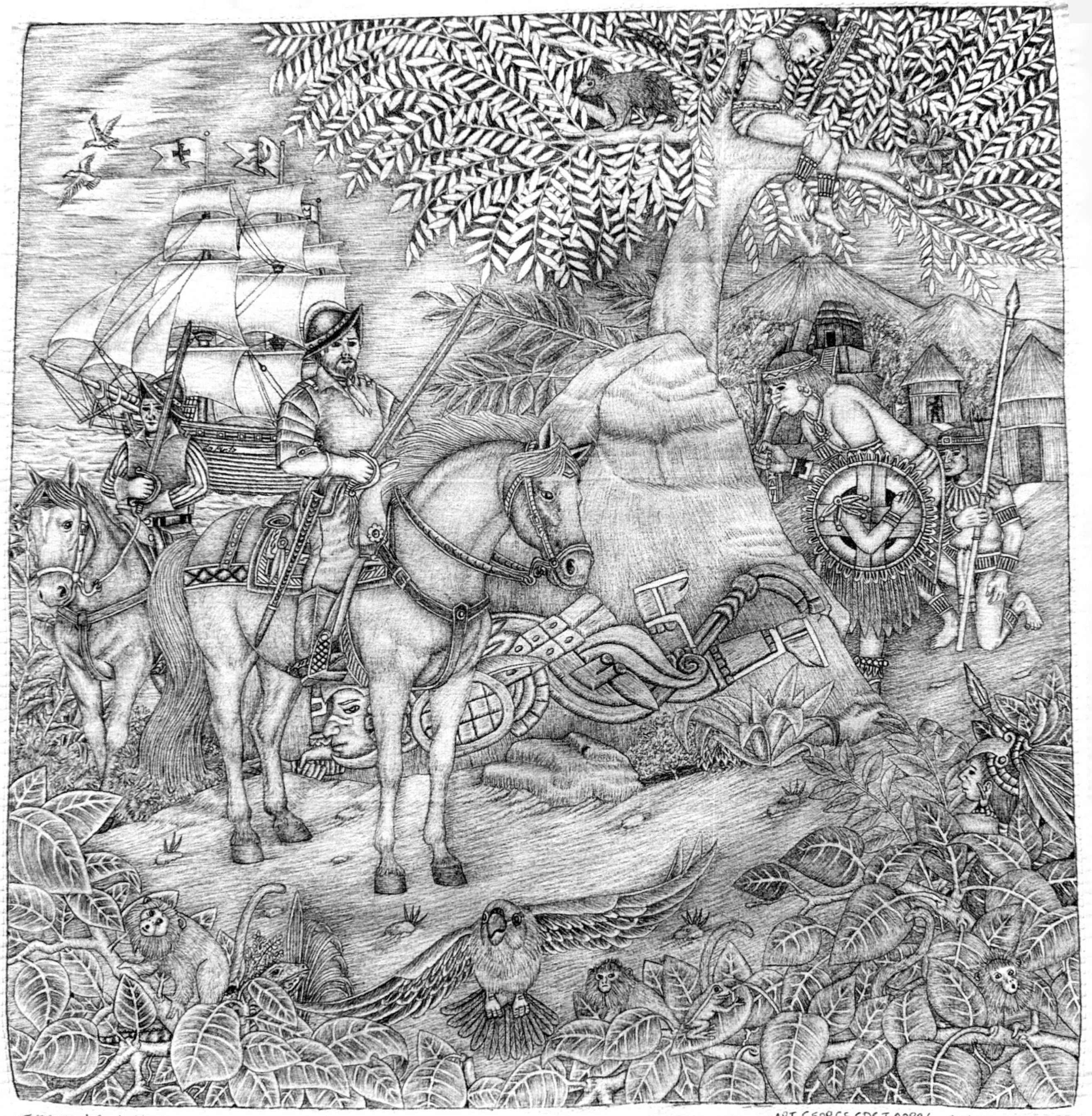

Ironwood State Prison

ART GEORGE CDC T-00826 9-16-23

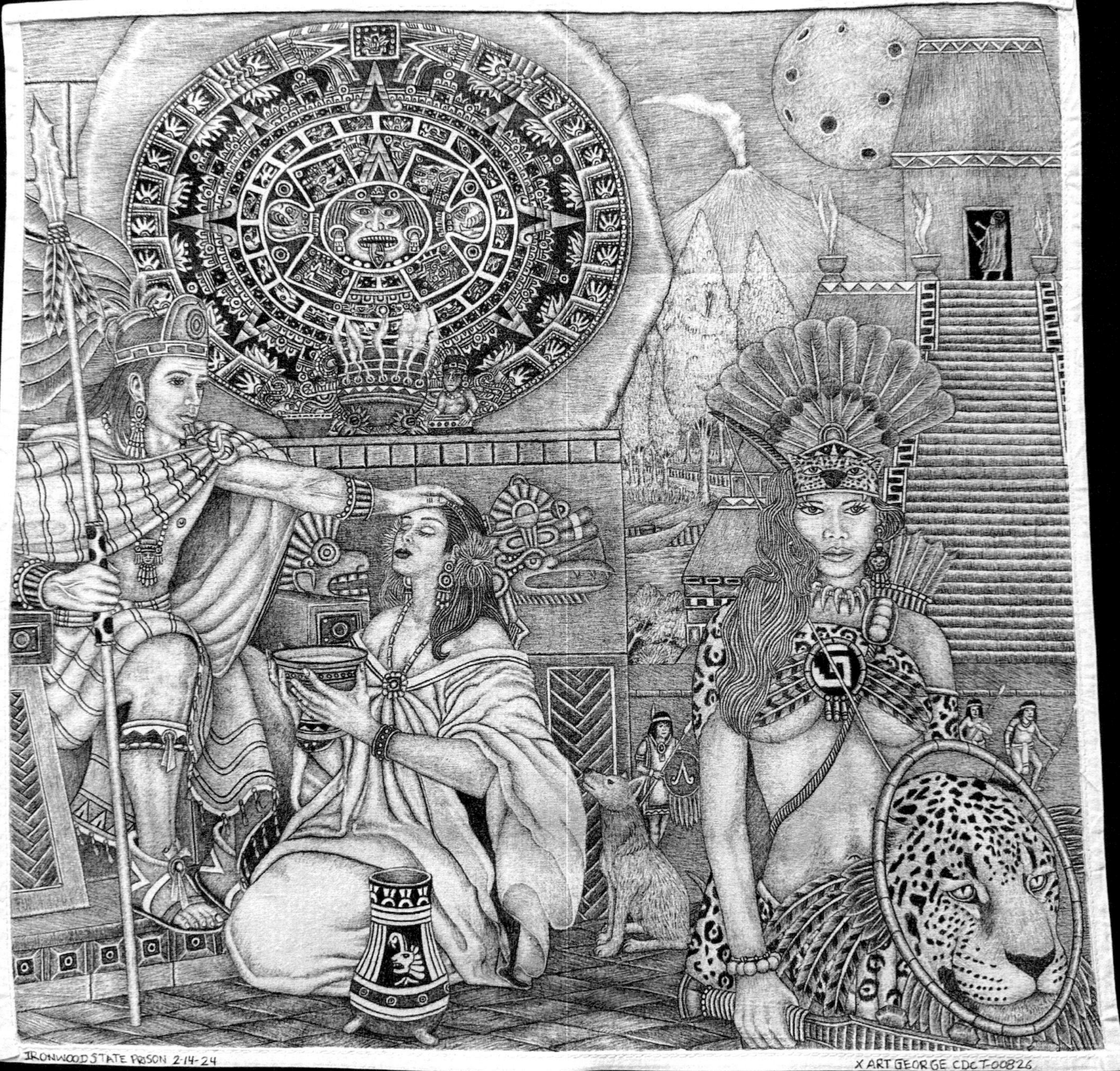
IRONWOOD STATE PRISON 2-14-24
X ART GEORGE CDCT-00826

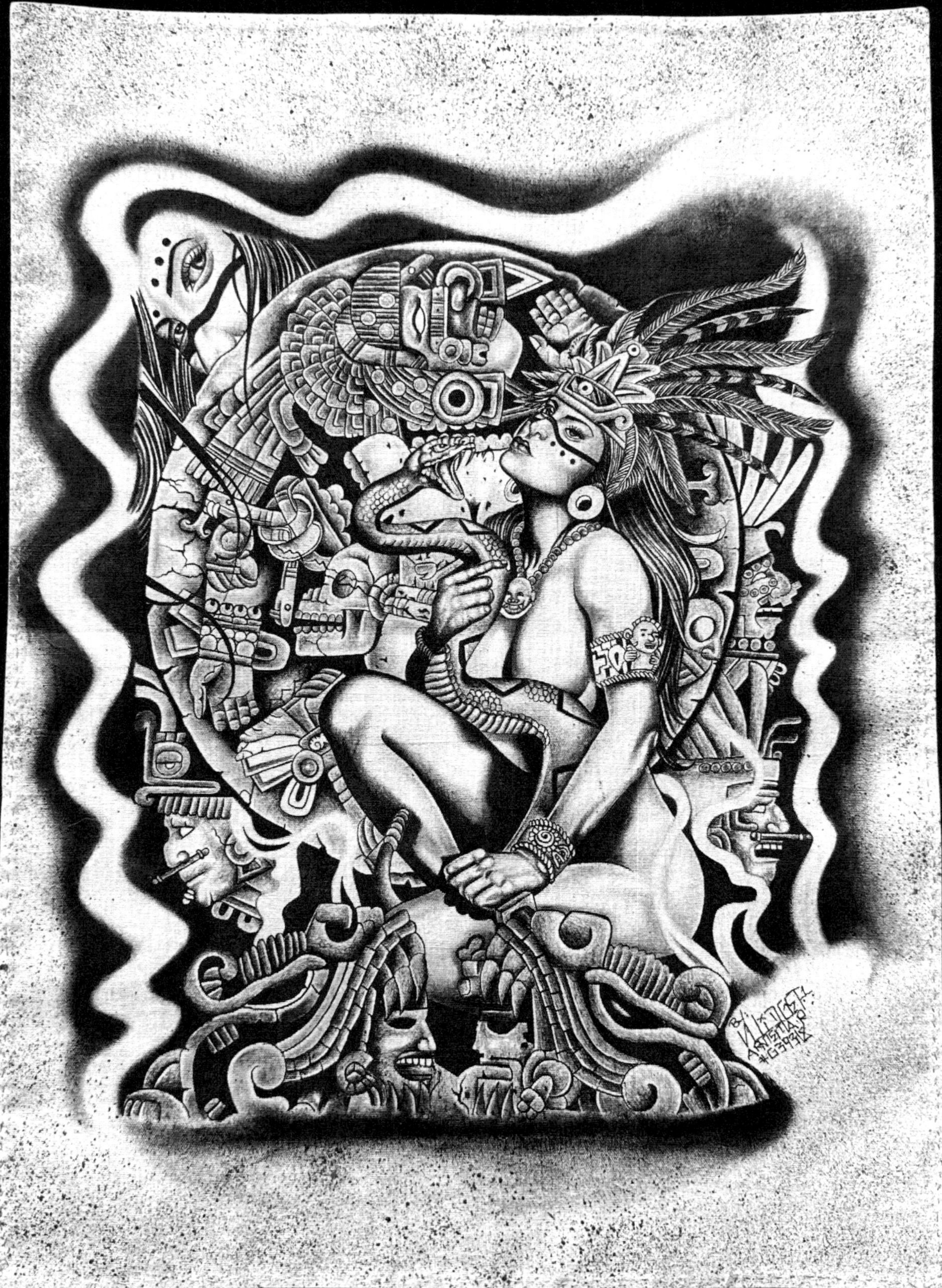
ARTISTA
#G39918

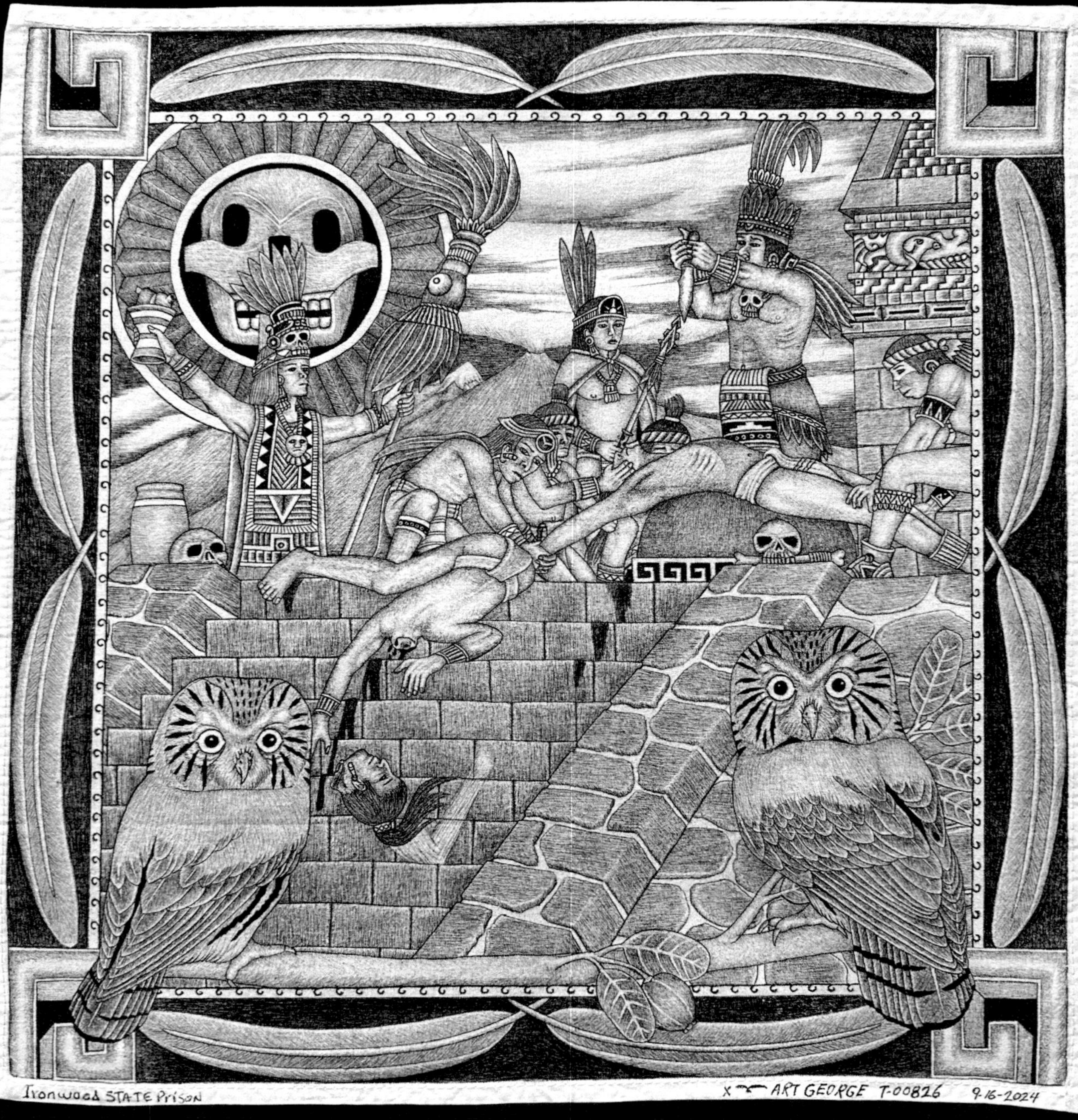
Ironwood STATE Prison
X ART GEORGE T-00826 9-16-2024

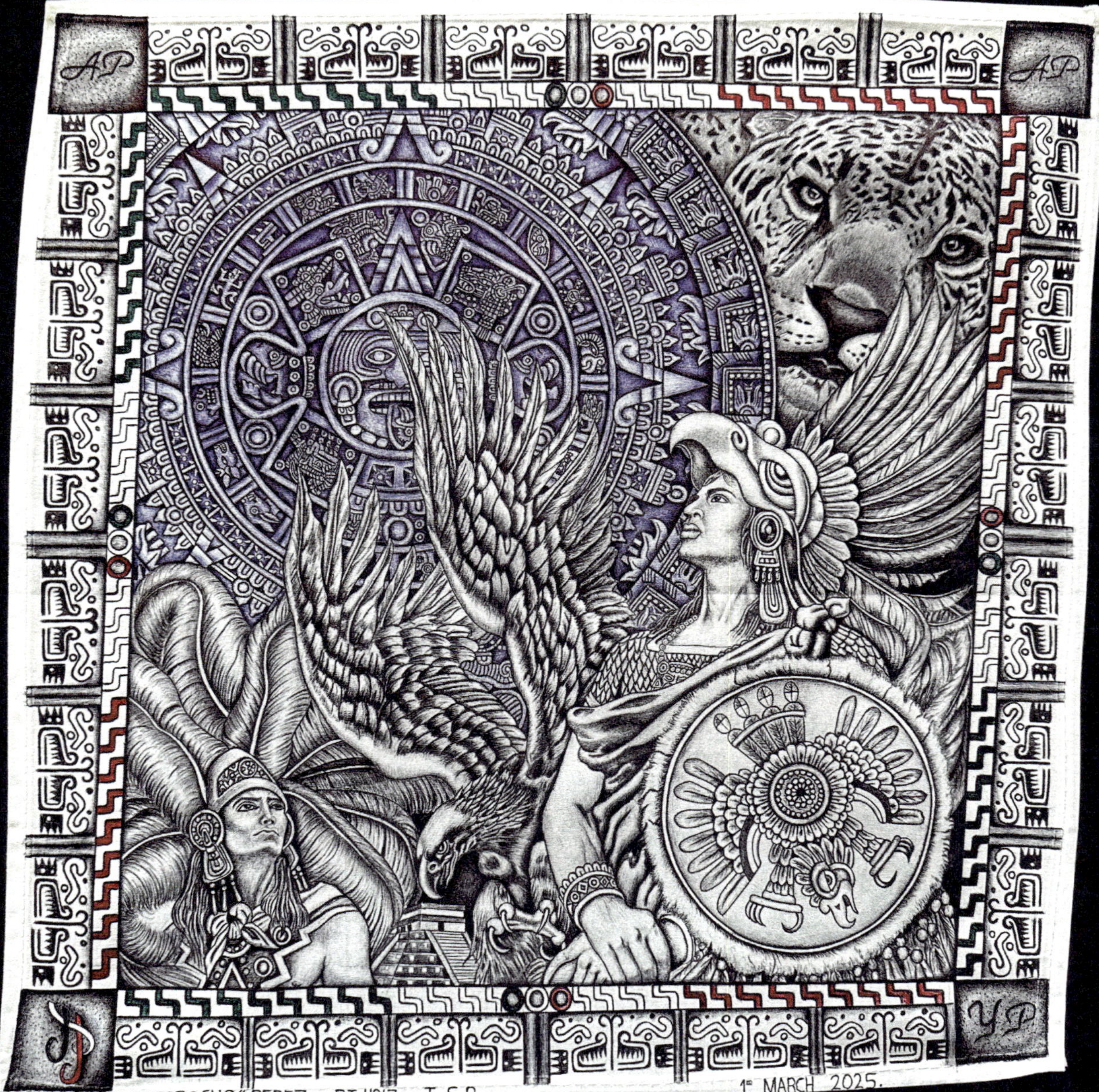

ALEJANDRO "JAROCHO" PEREZ BI 4817 I.S.P. 1st MARCH 2025.

ERIC “SUPERMAN” STURGESS

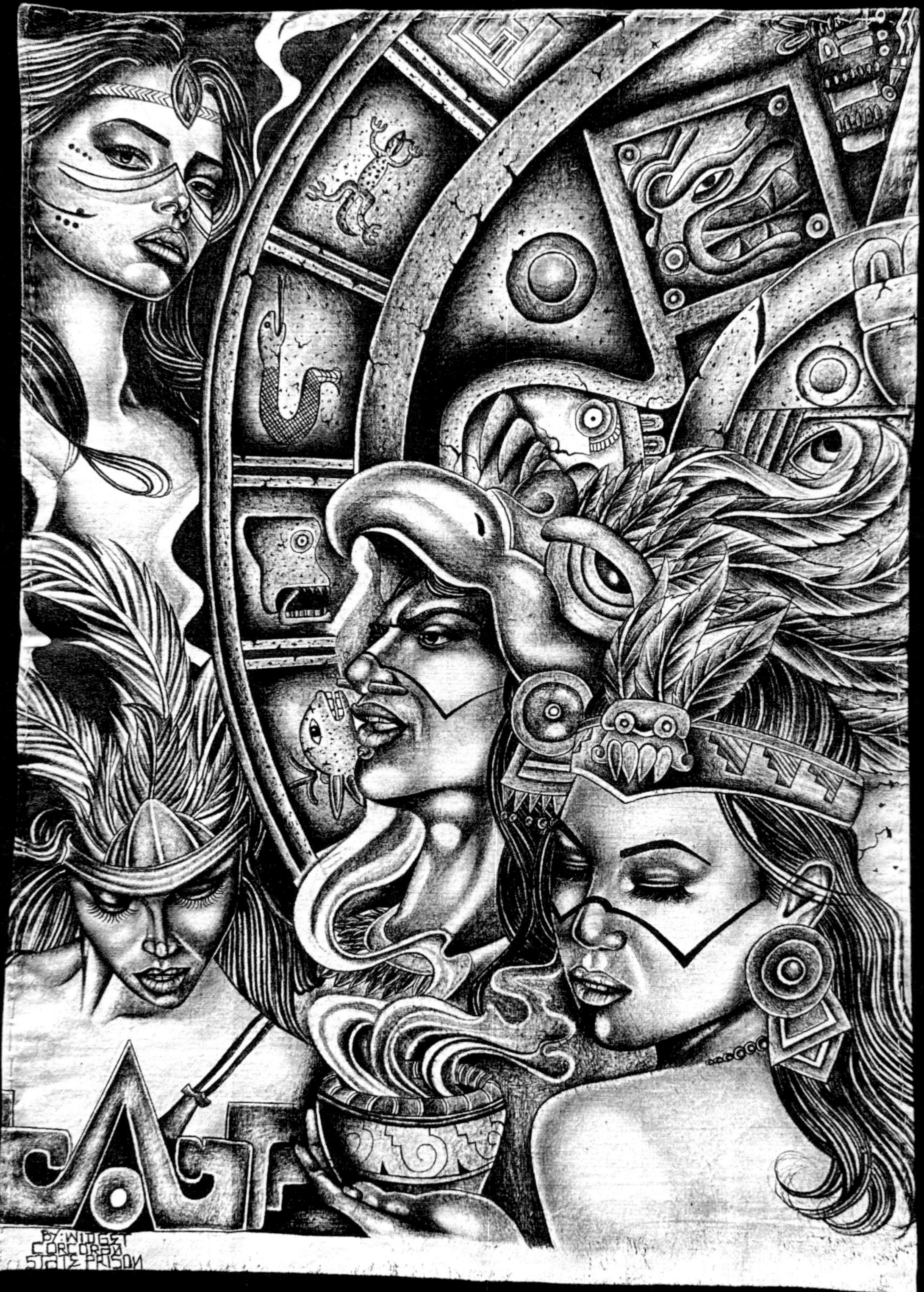

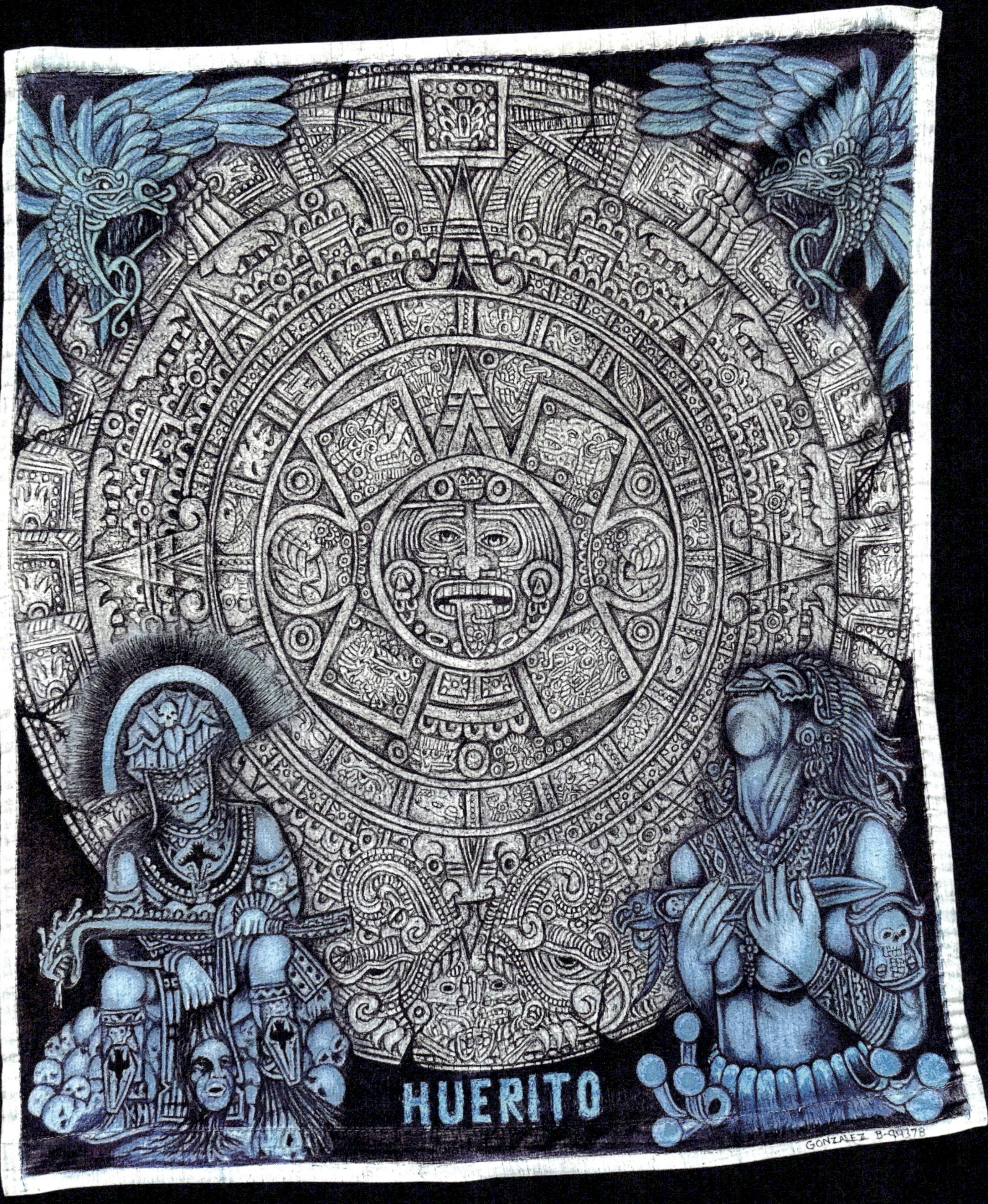
HUERITO
GONZALEZ B-99378

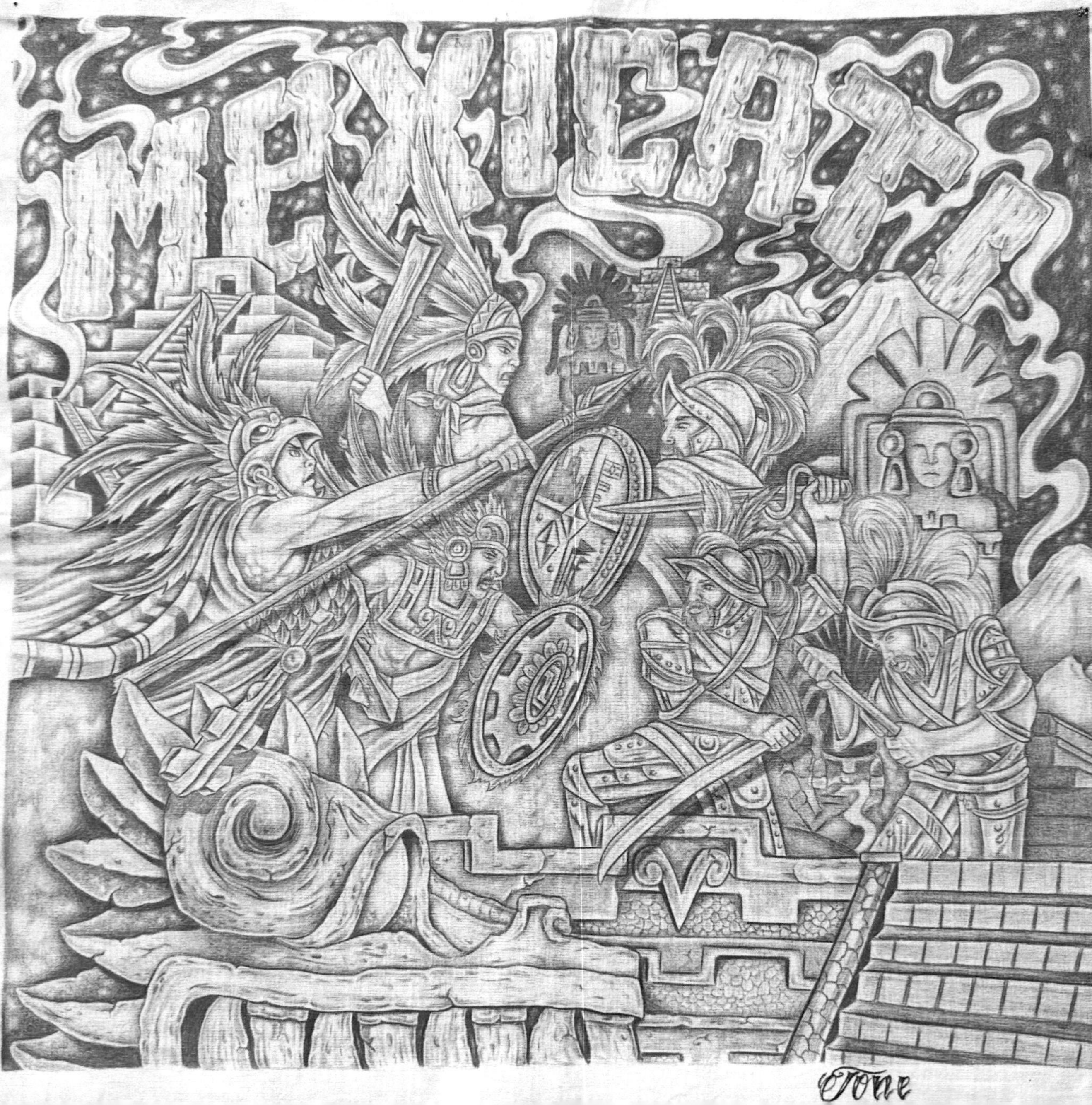
MEXICATL
Tone

About the Author

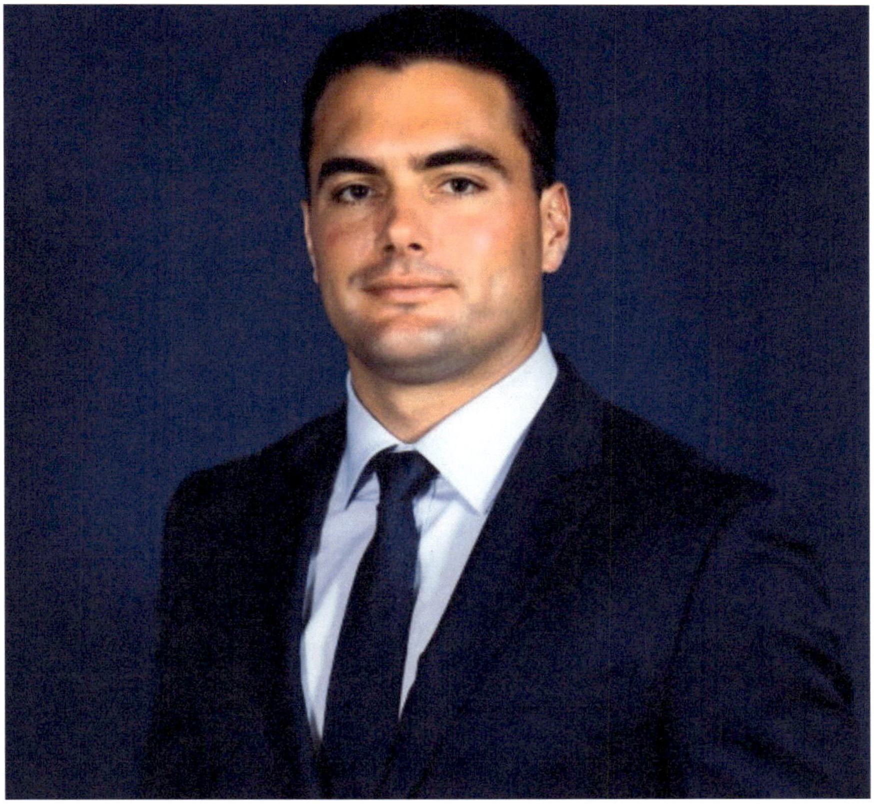

Eric has emerged as a highly accomplished investor and Day Trader, engaging in trading activities with a substantial value of stocks annually. He enjoys the status of a dedicated husband and father, being blessed with four wonderful daughters who hold a special place in his heart. Eric's existence revolves around upholding the virtues of a devout Christian, a devoted husband, and a caring father guided by the grace of God. His journey has been transformative, considering his challenging upbringing, and he now stands as an illustrious testament to the boundless possibilities achievable through faith in God.

Eric joined a criminal street gang as a teenager, and he was eventually arrested and put in a cage at the Long Beach City Jail. He dropped out of Jordan High School in Long Beach, California, in the 10th grade. Eric eventually got on the right path by the grace of God and obtained his GED the same month that he would have graduated. He joined the United States Coast Guard at 18, and after four years of faithful service, he was honorably discharged.

The following is an excerpt from his autobiography: "California Prison Confessions." "It was a typical beautiful summer night in Long Beach, California, and the three young teens fighting in the musty garage starkly contrasted the night's serenity. A teen called Bones was thrown against a wall, and a muscular teenager nicknamed E Double (me) rushed towards him and violently punched him in his lower back. Another youth named Tim Loc held Bones against the wall during this attack. E Double's knuckles landed with a thick-sounding thud as Bones grimaced and moaned in pain from each successive blow.

There's a look of pain and fear in Bone's eyes as E Double mercilessly lands blow after blow to his kidneys. E Double has spent years hitting the heavy bag in his garage, so his punches are devastating for his age. The beating lasted a minute, and the two teens stopped attacking the unfortunate victim. Amazingly, they all shook hands and embraced each other. We were all friends, and this was our modest gang initiation into our small clique called 'Six Feet Under.'"

Our tiny neighborhood gang in North Long Beach, California, had several members of various races: White, Black, and Hispanic. The definition of a criminal street gang according to the California Penal Code is as follows: "As used in this chapter, 'criminal street gang' means any ongoing organization, association, or group of three or more persons, whether formal or informal, having as one of its primary activities the commission of one or more of the criminal acts…having a common name or common identifying sign or symbol, and whose members individually or collectively engage in or have engaged in a pattern of criminal gang activity," California Penal Code 186.22(f).

Some of our associates committed serious crimes such as burglaries, drug sales, stealing cars, carrying guns, vandalism, and assaulting people. Although we were nothing but young punks, we were a criminal street gang according to the California Penal Code.

The FBI did a study entitled "Street-Gang Mentality: A Mosaic of Remorseless Violence and Relentless Loyalty." I want to quote a relevant part concerning young males who do not have a father or other positive male role models in their lives while growing up: "All gang members lacked male role models in their households, and when they lived with their mothers, they were rarely home because of work schedules. Gang members often lived temporarily with various people. All but one gang member reported that one or more immediate family members had a criminal history or abused drugs. Gangs attracted them because of their loyalty, stability, and sense of group identity."

There is an epidemic in this country of boys masquerading as men who don't take their responsibilities as fathers seriously. Many fathers aren't involved in their children's lives; if they are, they are a horrible example of what a real man should be. One of the main factors in young men ending up in the penal system is the lack of a father or, at the very least, a positive male role model when they were growing up. Absentee fathers are causing society to pay a high price for their selfish and callous actions.

Every day, I strive to be the best dad to the four beautiful daughters God has blessed me with. I live by the motto, "Be the man you needed as a child." I will not allow the actions of physically and emotionally abusive people to define who I am or hinder my advancement in life. You can choose to be bitter or better. I strive for excellence because living well is the best response to abusive people.

Eric Sturgess

God bless you and yours.

Romans 10:9-13

For those seeking to connect with Eric or gather additional insights about his upcoming projects, please visit his official website: EricSturgess.com.

Other Books

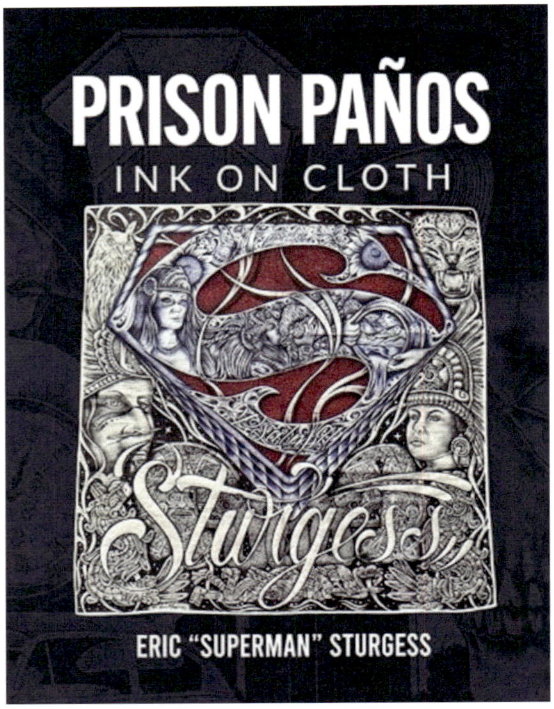

Prison Paños: Ink On Cloth

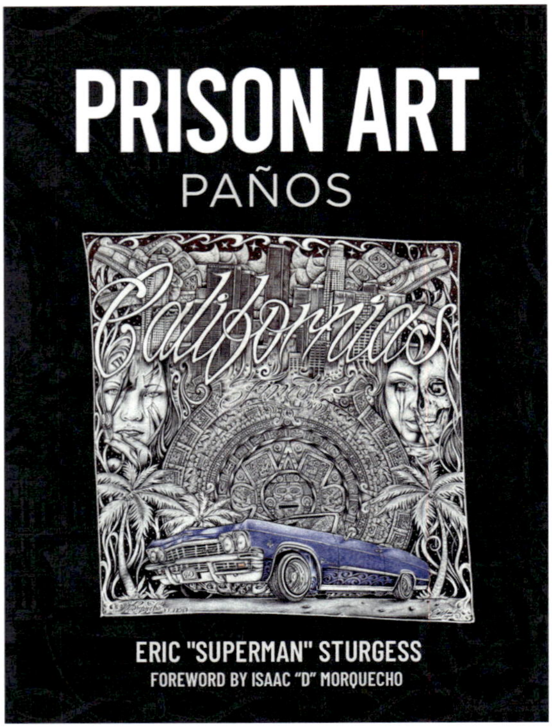

Prison Art Paños

Prison Art Hats

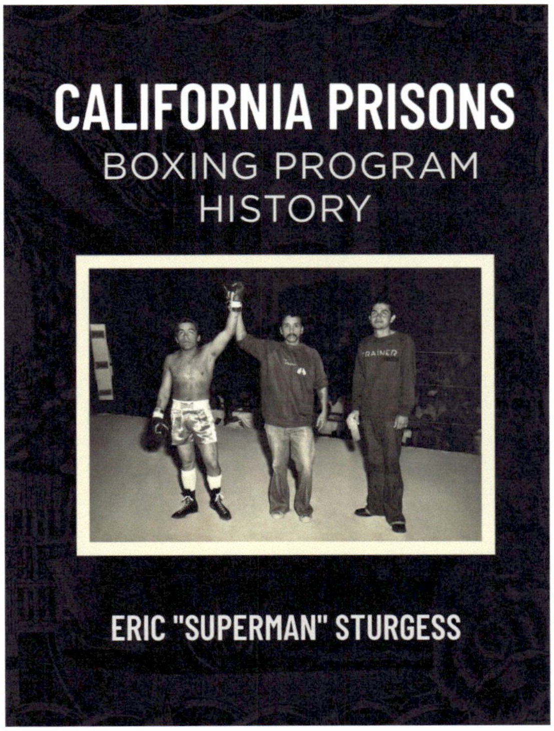

California Prisons:
Boxing Program History

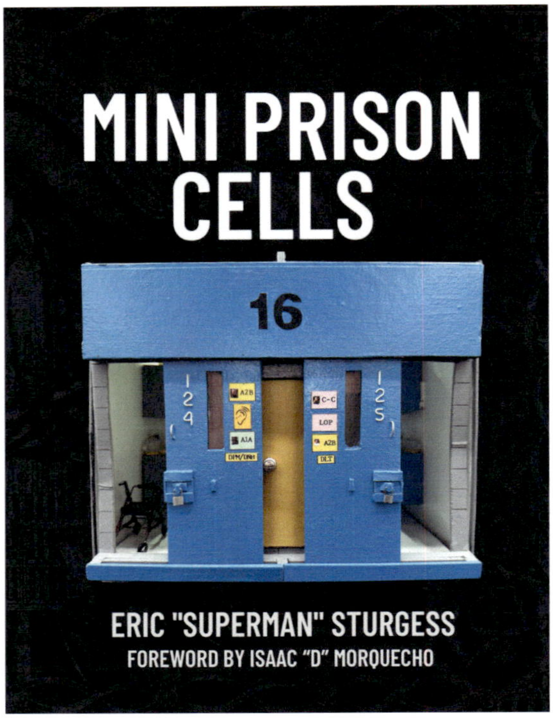

Mini Prison Cells

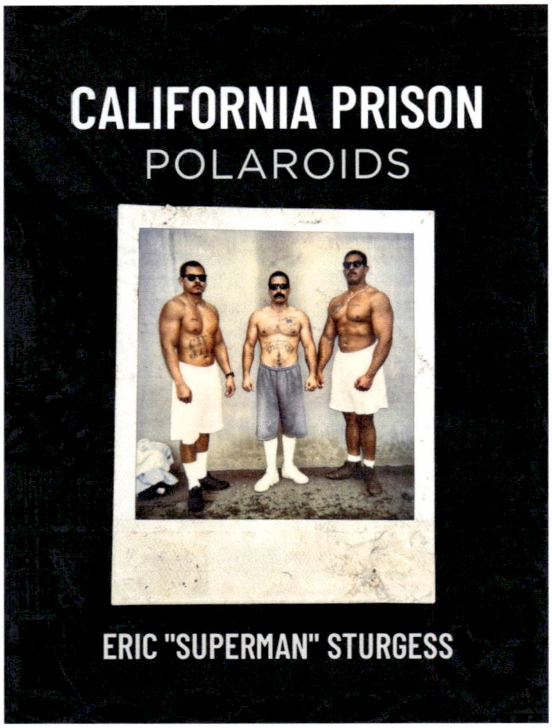

California Prison Polaroids

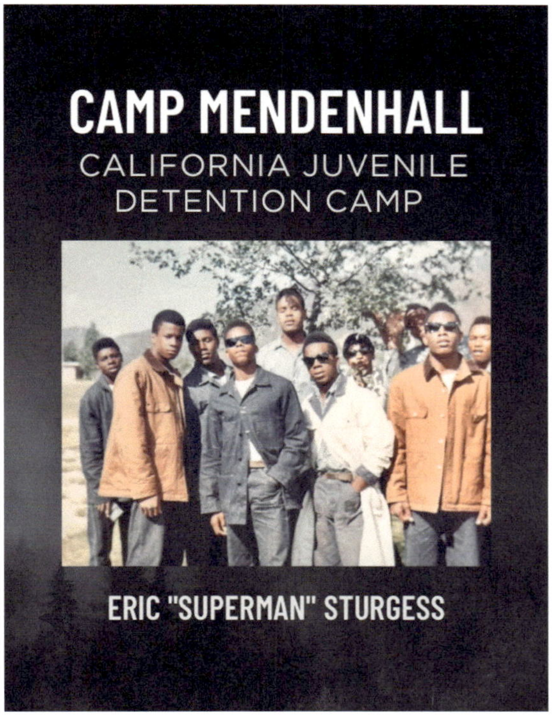

Camp Mendenhall: California Juvenile Detention Camp

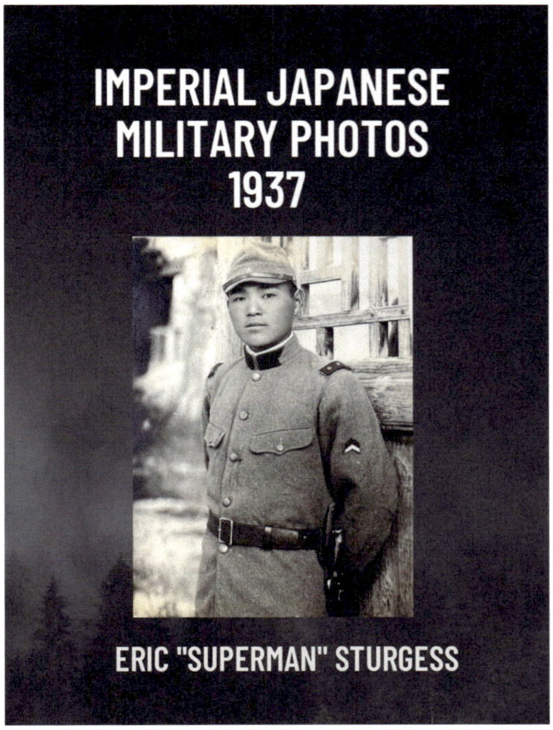

Imperial Japanese Military Photos 1937

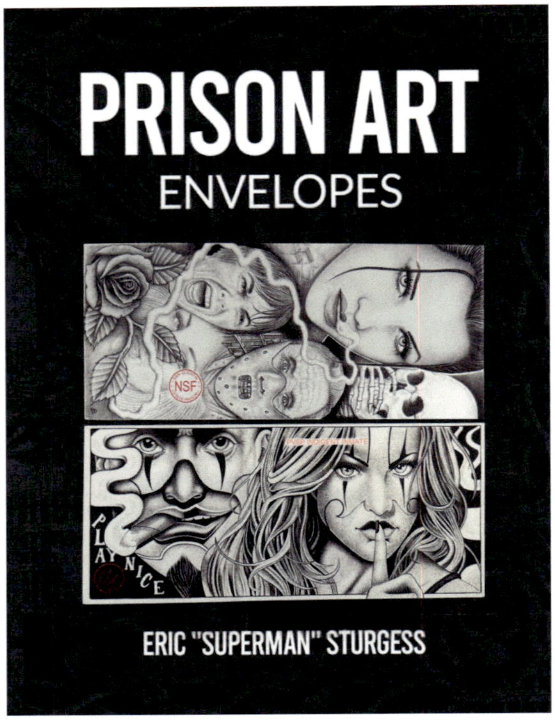

Prison Art Envelopes

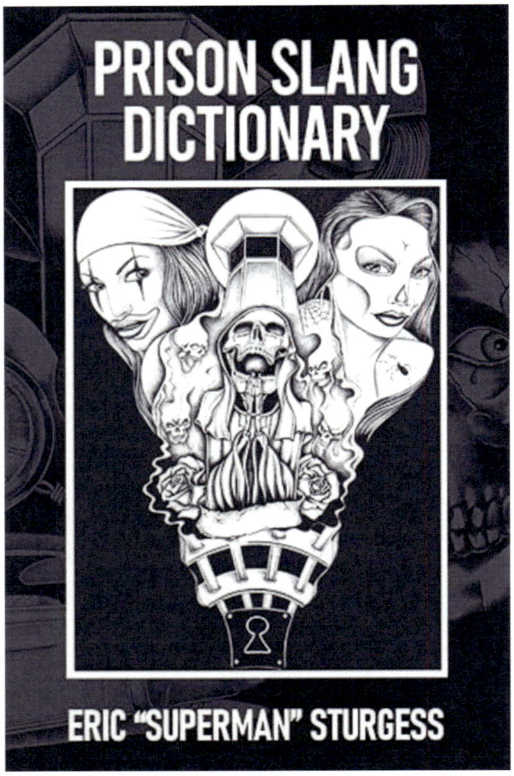

Prison Slang Dictionary

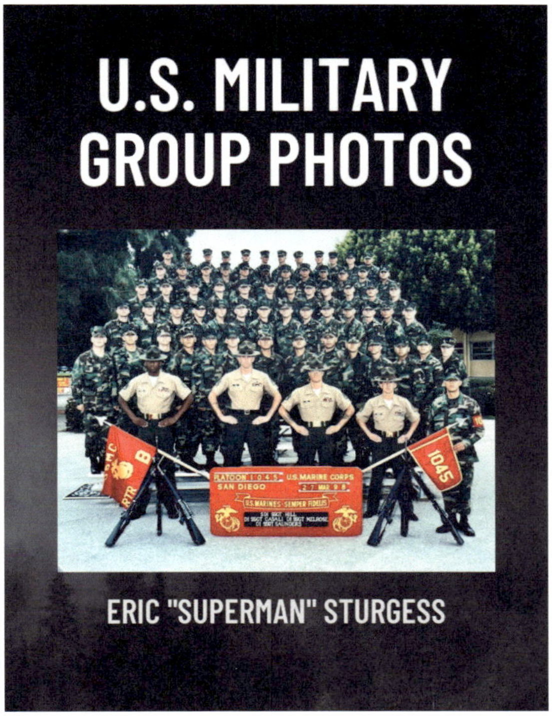

U.S. Military Group Photos

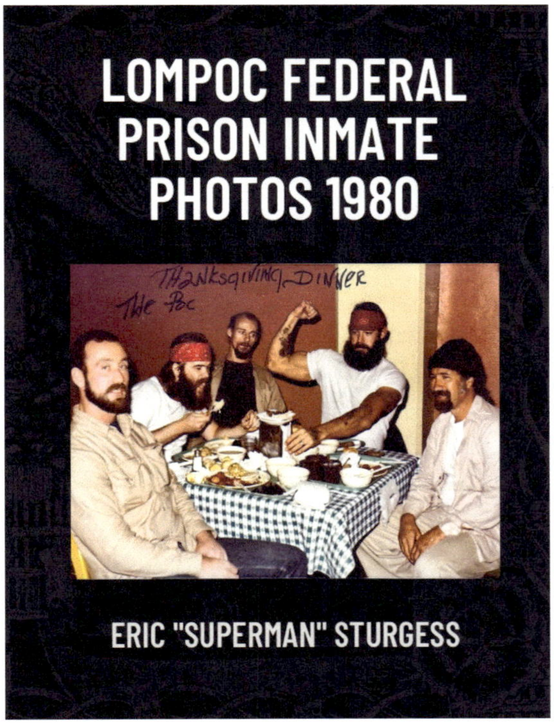

Lompoc Federal Prison Inmate Photos 1980

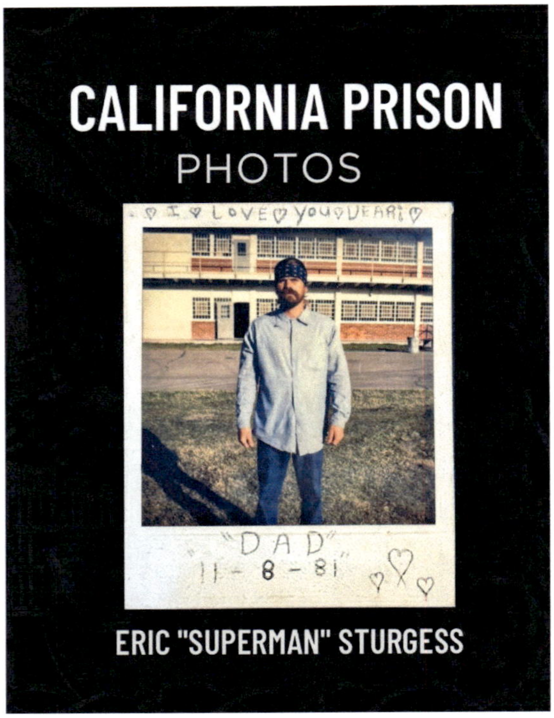

California Prison Photos

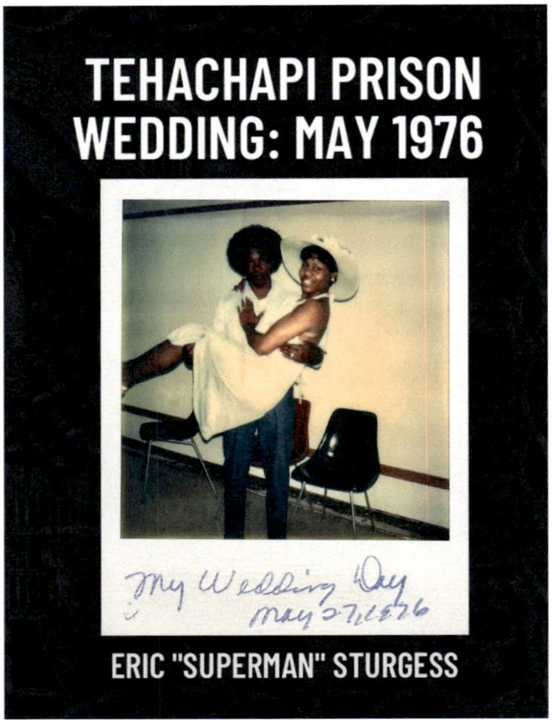

Tehachapi Prison
Wedding: May 1976

Made in the USA
Las Vegas, NV
09 November 2026

57764361R00038